The
Pictorial History of
Trucks

The Pictorial History of **Trucks**

Eric Gibbins & Graeme Ewens

CHARTWELL BOOKS INC.

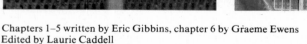

Chapters 1–5 written by Eric Gibbins, chapter 6 by Graeme Ewens
Edited by Laurie Caddell
Orbis Publishing is indebted to IVECO for allowing us to use their photographs in this book.
We are also grateful to the RMC Group for letting us photograph the Hall & Co vehicles

Published by Chartwell Books Inc.,
A Division of Books Sales Inc.,
110 Enterprise Avenue, Secaucus, N.J. 07094
ISBN 0–89009–204–4
Library of Congress Catalog Card Number: 78–53454
Printed in Spain by General Grafic

Picture Acknowledgments

B. Babcock/Orbis: 43 – Bedford: 148c – Black Star: 99b, 100c – N. Bruce: 64 – B. Chalker/Orbis:
132-133 – Columbia Pictures: 155 – Daimler Benz: 25a, 26b and c, 27 – I. Dawson: 135b –
G. Ewens: 16a & b, 17a & b, 110, 131c, 136a, 144b, 145a – Fiat: 54b, 76b, 102 – Foden: 22, 25b,
56, 79c, 96c – Ford: 40a, 108c – E. Gibbins: 24, 29b, 35b, 53b, 107, 116 – GMC: 34, 40b, 61a,
82b, 117, 120 – 121, 138 – 139 – Hillcrest Motor Co/Orbis: 43 – Robert Hunt Picture Library:
36-37, 49b, 92, 96a, 104 – Imperial War Museum: 61b & c, 99a – International: 31a, 55, 115b,
146d, 152, 153c – Isuzu: 154 – IVECO: 8, 9a & b, 11, 14 15, 29a, 30, 35a, 36, 38, 45, 57, 59, 75,
83, 119, 127, 128, 145b, 150-151, 153a & b, Leyland: 23, 46, 53a, 70, 71b, 74a, 122c,·142 –
Magirus Deutz: 148 – MAN: 77a & b – A. Morland: 9c, 10, 16c, 136b, 137, 141 & b, 146a & b –
Musée National des Techniques: 20-21b & c – National Film Archives: 131a & b, 134, 146b & c
– National Motor Museum: 18 19, 28b, 32 – 33, 39, 44b, 49a, 51, 58c, 61d, 68, 71a, 72a & c, 76a,
79b, 82a, 84b, 89, 92c, 106, 112-113, 114 – Old Motor: 44a, 52, 54a & c, 58a & b, 62, 63b, 69a
& b – Olyslager: 88 – Orbis 20-21a, d & e, 26a, 94 & b, 118, 135a, 148b – Peterbilt: 115a –
Renault: 49c, 124a, 143a – Roadrunner Productions: 141c, 146a – Scania: 77c, 124b –
J. Spencer Smith/Orbis: 50, 69c, 79a, 84a, 86 – 87, 96b – Truck: 143b – Ullstein: 100b – USIS:
90 – USNA: 100a, 108b – Volvo: 108a, 122 – Westlong Trucks: 80 – 81 – White: 6-7 –
N. Wright/Orbis: 12 – 13, 17c, 40c, 63a & c, 67, 72b & d, 74b, 78, 82c, 144a

Front cover photograph by Ian Dawson
Back cover photographs: Bryan Chalker/Orbis, National Motor Museum, Andrew Morland
Endpapers: Ian Dawson
Title page: J. Spencer Smith/Orbis

Contents

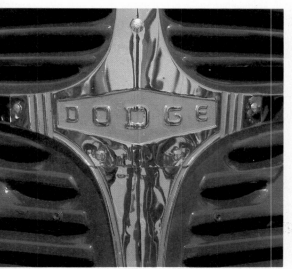

Introduction

There was a time, not so very long ago, when the romance of the railroad gripped America: a time when railroading people, from the legendary Casey Jones to the infamous Jesse James, were regarded by the common man in a way akin to hero worship; a time when every small boy, even in areas unserved by the expanding rail network, dreamed of becoming an engineer and a time when music, rhyme and fiction seemed to centre on one subject alone – the story of the 'iron road'. This was America at the end of the nineteenth Century, in a period when it was still relatively young and still a continent of adventurers seeking the benefits of gold, oil and agriculture. With government and big business stimulation, the railroad had opened up vast tracts of previously uninhabited land, encouraged the establishment of new settlements and, more than anything else, sped the movement of passengers and freight to such an extent that the pony express and stagecoach became obsolete overnight. The railroad, however, had one major fault. Even though it did play a major role in the distribution of passengers and freight, the final delivery point was rarely at the railhead and to transfer passengers and freight to horse-drawn transport seemed to cancel the railroad's advantages.

What was needed was a compromise between the railroad's speed and efficiency and the so far unequalled flexibility of the horse. The solution came from Europe in the form of the self-propelled motor vehicle. As developments in the automotive field spread through Europe, so New World inventors worked on their own ideas, culminating in the unveiling of Charles Duryea's first automobile in 1892, what is generally regarded as the first American self-propelled vehicle. Within ten years, the first

Left: the truck has come a long way on the road of development in its eighty year history

American freight truck, a 'horseless buggie' coupled to a previously horse-drawn wagon, signalled the start of the next American revolution and the dawn of the latest American legend: the long-haul trucker.

Initially, there was scepticism on all sides. Objections from the horse-loving fraternity were many, from those with a financial interest in rail-roading numerous and often voluble, and from a government which had also backed the rail network there was little or no encouragement. In many ways, problems such as these generated an even greater spirit of adventure and achievement and, with hard campaigning and highly exhaustive and often dangerous public testing and other promotional schemes, the American trucking industry took its first faltering steps. The development of commercial road transport was worldwide but there was no better proving ground than the vast American continent with its climatic and regional extremes.

Just as the railroad gave birth to its folk heroes back in the 1800s, so trucking spawned its own characters and began to display its own brand of excitement and glamour. Truck driving, even in the early days, was becoming the vocation for the cowboy, the former railroader and the adventurer. There were no steel rails to guide the vehicle and in many regions there were no roads at all; also there was certainly no comfort. As a trucker, you were at the mercy of the weather, you sat on rough boards, you drove over unmade ground, there were no truck stops and you either slept under the vehicle or in amongst the freight, whatever that may have been!

Truck design changed dramatically during the first half of the century: from an engine-under-seat layout at the turn of the century, through bonneted and cab-beside-engine arrangements, to the 'cabover' and 'conventional' designs of the 1950s '60s and '70s, virtually every combination has been tried and one is inclined to wonder where we shall go from here. Just as engine/cab arrangements have changed, so too have the engines themselves. Brief interest in steam in the very early days soon changed to gasoline, with the close proximity of readily available supplies, and then to the more economical diesel. Since then, engine horsepower has increased, new lightweight materials such as aluminium have been incorporated in engine design and an even lighter power unit, the gas turbine, has been tried. So far, however, the turbine has been uneconomical in operation.

With the advent of diesel propulsion came the first major increase in 'red tape': the 1935

Left: four versions of cab design from 1903, 1923, 1953 and 1973. In that time, things have got a lot easier for the drivers who now sit in comfort at their lightweight controls in air conditioned luxury. Of course, the earliest cabs were air conditioned but in a rather different manner

Below: perhaps the image of the trucker as a modern day cowboy is not such an exaggerated cliché after all

9

Motor Carriers Act, which sought to establish control of interstate road haulage but in fact enabled big business to take over control, hiring and firing drivers at will, and engaging in corruption or worse. It proved to be a great error to attempt to limit the trucker's freedom, as it was this very same freedom and sense of adventure that had put him on the road in the first place. Lessons are not learned easily in government circles and, by 1940, a public health service study had recommended the introduction of a ten hour driving day.

To save time and money, drivers were sleeping with their trucks even more than before and, with the new regulations, a two man crew became commonplace on long-haul work so that one drove while the other slept. Rapidly, the sleeper cab, at first known as a 'suicide box', became established located behind the cab or even beneath the chassis; these have now developed into the monster double sleeper cabs.

It was not only the regulations that changed during the 1930s. After the Depression, when many truckers and others went to the wall, some form of rejuvenation was needed. It came in the form of lavish styling throughout the automotive field, not only for the private automobile but for the truck as well, and continued apace right into the 1950s. Fashionable trends included bulbous all-enveloping fenders, chromium-plating everywhere and extra fins, styling strips, lights and other paraphernalia.

By the 1950s, it had become apparent to every inter-state trucker that length and weight restrictions imposed by individual states were confusing to say the least; by 1978, this problem had reached unmanagable proportions resulting in the inter-stater spending as much time on bureaucratic paperwork and checking his legality as he did actually driving. Certain states, such as Oregon, permit double or triple-bottom outfits comprising one tractor, a

Right: forward and normal control versions on Kenworth chassis. The bonneted normal control outfit has much more room for the sleeper cab, whereas the cab-over-engine vehicle gives the driver a better view of the road. The Old El Paso rig is one of the many vehicles hired out by the Hertz corporation

semi-trailer and one or two drawbar trailers, whilst other states allow only one semi-trailer. Elsewhere, axle loadings are so prohibitive (in Michigan, for example) that what would resemble a near normal rig in one state is forced to carry a row of multi-axles to distribute the load in another.

Design problems such as this have resulted in such complicated specifications for US-built trucks that there is now no such thing as a standard heavy duty over-the-road model. When a new range is launched, it normally comprises both convential and cabover variations with these sub-divided into hundreds of options, sometimes offering as many as ten engine specifications and as many or even more for transmission, brakes, steering and even cab. Outwardly, modern rigs may look similar, but look beneath the surface and a host of differences will become apparent.

Not only are the regulations different between states, but truckers themselves can be divided into categories. Compare a trucker from the eastern seaboard with his opposite number from the West Coast, and some surprises will be in store. The eastern man is invariably a steady worker, more often than not in the employ of a freight or van line, toiling hard to earn a reasonable living. He dresses in ordinary working clothes and is glad to get home at night to be with his family. The Westerner, on the other hand, is often the image of the real American cowboy, right down to cowboy boots, Stetson hat and denims. He could well be an independent trucker, an owner-operator, proud to have his own machine and eager to move. His outgoing personality is reflected in his truck, often festooned with 'gingerbread' (chromium-plating, extra lights, decals, gleaming paint finish and anything else that might attract attention). He would rather be on the road than at home – indeed, his truck is his home. There are, of course, exceptions to the rule but

Left: intercontinental trucking is now an integral part of long-distance hauling, especially with the greatly increased trade in the mid 1970s with the Arabian countries. Here, a row of Milanese 170 Fiats lead a DT Ford through Asia

this stereotyping is based on good evidence in the trucking world.

The 1970s have seen yet more design changes, not for the sake of change but as an economy measure. Many fleet users have adopted the use of aerofoils attached to cab roofs or specially contoured plastic pods that locate over the front bulkheads of semi-trailer vans. It has been found that these methods aid fuel economy by lessening wind resistance, and engine drivers have even been able to introduce fuel saving into the power unit itself. So great is the proof that aerodynamic alterations lead to fuel economy that General Motors now offers an aerofoil as an option for its 'Astro' range, and both Mack and Kenworth have announced a double-deck sleeper with contoured roof line which also acts as a wind spoiler. There can be little doubt that aerodynamics and the use of ideas and materials developed in the aerospace industry will be deployed in future truck design. Already there are futuristic prototypes from Chevrolet and Ryder Truck Rental with deeper and wider windshields, space-age instrumentation, more rounded contours and recessed lights. Production versions are not due to appear for a number of years, however. Meantime, what can a trucker do to cover vehicle purchase, where a superbly finished handbuilt Western tractor unit can cost up to $60,000 plus. One solution which has been around for some time but only now, with rapidly escalating costs, is catching on fast is the use of 'glider kits'. By using such a kit, an existing long-haul truck, possibly with one million miles on the clock, can be re-built to the latest specification, incorporating the most up-to-date legal requirements and costing exactly half the price of a brand new model. At that sort of discount, who could complain?

The trucking industry now handles more freight than any other transport medium in the United States. The inflexibility of the railroad has long since lost the race. Much of this has been due to the construction of a vast Interstate Highway System which has not only affected the railroad but also another trucking phenomenon, the truck-stop.

As recently as the 1930s, truck-stops were few and far between, and washing or sleeping facilities virtually unheard of. Trucking was an extension of life in the Old West where, instead of riding from saloon to saloon as the cowboy had done, the trucker plotted his course from fuel point to fuel point and, like his ancestors, slept under the stars and bathed out in the open, too.

With ever increasing numbers of trucks crossing the American continent, others were quick to realise the potential of these facilities. Existing service stations were amongst the first to cash in, with 'Pa' servicing the vehicles and 'Ma' dishing up the food. Larger concerns, particularly the oil companies, opened complete service areas where the trucker could purchase all his requirements, and some existing roadhouses provided additional facilities for the trucker. Some, of course, were rip-offs, while others could not have given better value for money

The introduction of the Interstate highway system was to sound the death knell for many of these places and also end, once and for all, the railroad's monopoly of long-haul freight movement. As the Interstate system has expanded so the trucker's status has improved. Slowly he has become a legend, operating in a world apart from the man in the street. The media has tended to exploit this world through music, TV, radio and even films. The trucker's own music is largely country & western, again with that feeling of the open air and freedom. Not only have recording stars put trucking on the map, but truckers have also become famous for their songs, and on occasions top pop personalities have also pushed the trucker's image still higher. Television series such as *Movin' On* seek to portray the trucker as an incorruptible hero – which goes a long way to boosting his image, largely at the expense of truth, however.

Radio stations throughout America often dedicate regular programmes to the lonely trucker, playing requests, messages and providing a specialist news service for the lonely men on the road whose only other comforts are the occasional 8-track stereo and a Citizen's Band radio. This, then, is the world of the heavy truck on long-haul work, shorter journey runs and on or off the road. A world where everything seems a little unreal unless it is your bread and butter – as a trucker.

The truck stop is the oasis at the end of each stint of hauling where drivers and trucks are rested, fed and cleaned. The truckers also have the benefit of female entertainment. . . Here, too, drivers can talk to each other without the need of CB radio and also where they can get a lift, below, should their truck give up the ghost. Should the vehicle expire anywhere else, however, the cost of getting an immaculate chrome-plated wrecker to your aid is enormously expensive

CHAPTER 1

The Early Days

The truck is a product of the twentieth century, and its history is also the story of the development of a modern technology. Whilst it parallels that of the motor car, the truck's evolution has obviously many facets peculiar to the function of goods carrying. Its early development owes something to the pioneers of steam-powered road vehicles, but there are many more relevant influences to take into account. However, before pinpointing the people, products and events which marked those first tottering steps to the modern truck, it is appropriate to take a look at the general picture which emerges of the commercial road transport scene in the first century and a quarter – from 1769 when the first mechanically propelled vehicle was driven on the roads.

The development of mechanical traction on public roads was a European affair and, to a large degree, an English one. England had the need for something better than the horse and, at the time, had the resources to provide it. Germany and France followed, but it was not until the twentieth century that America came into the picture. Second, inland transport during the nineteenth century was totally dominated by the railways. What road traction there was revolved around the continuous and pressing need for increased efficiency in agriculture. That was something which meant steam power which, in turn, was most conveniently supplied by a self propelling traction engine. Only a handful of inventors persisted with the design of load carrying vehicles, or trucks, and in fact the truck did not make its debut until the 1890s.

Scrutiny of both the earliest period and the years following reveals the history of trucks as a power struggle. It is a record of a contest initially between the steam engine and the horse (which steam lost), then steam versus the petrol engine (which steam lost again) and, finally, the slow but steady eclipse of petrol by the apparently unconquerable diesel. However, to attribute all the changes that have taken place to one major component – albeit a major one – is perhaps an over simplification but, without the engine, there would have been no comparable development in gearboxes and transmissions and the advances in chassis and body design which go to make up the truck of today.

There are constant reminders that economic development of trucks has stemmed from advances in engine technology, efficiency and power levels. However, a secondary power struggle is also apparent which may at times seem to overshadow all other influences. This is the battle between the truck engineer, the public and opposing interests which have ranged over the years from landowners to providers of other forms of transport – especially the railways – and from government legislation to the environmental lobby.

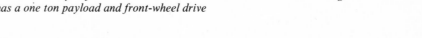

This 1896 Thornycroft steamer is the oldest commercial vehicle in running order in Britain; it has a one ton payload and front-wheel drive

In the early part of the nineteenth century, the horse was supreme and remained so on the roads for the remainder of the century. The development of mechanical road transport vehicles was not encouraged in many parts of the world; in fact, quite the reverse happened. Attempts to establish road passenger and goods services with steam-powered or drawn vehicles were actively fought by legislation, city fathers, landowners and other vested interests. The day of the environmentalist and conservationist was about to dawn but perhaps then there was much greater justification for the fears of the populace about the running of these fearsome-seeming juggernauts – in view of their brakes (or lack of them), their instability, and the nuisance of their noise, smoke and sparks – than there is today with the giant, multi-wheeled, but very safe, diesel-powered articulated outfits.

Because the horse was the accepted form of transport in the nineteenth century, the argument that mechanical vehicles 'frightened the horses' was used at every turn to frustrate the attempts to run mechanical road vehicles by the early pioneers of this form of transport. Opposition to the mechanical road vehicle was on grounds of noise, excessive smoke emission, road damage and general safety, and there was also a huge investment in terms of both finance and manpower in horse-based transport systems. This resulted in punitive legislation against it in many countries, particularly Britain, which undoubtedly checked its advance for several decades. Much was made of accidents involving steering failure, vehicles over-turning and vehicles blowing up – all of which created an adverse climate of public opinion.

The first 'trucks' were steam designs, pioneered by the famous vehicle built by Frenchman Nicholas Cugnot. In fact, he and Englishmen Trevithick, Watt and Murdoch built some of the first road vehicles of any sort. Their steam drags were cumbersome and ungainly but, in their construction, the designers found out a lot about suspension and steering, even if their power units were a step up a dead end street. The lessons learnt were not to be wasted in later years, though. Road conditions also provided a natural limitation on speeds and there were many incidents where rocks and other obstructions were placed in the path of steam wagons to make their movement even more difficult. Moreover, while road steamers could on the whole travel faster (attaining speeds of 15 to 20mph), the speeds attainable were nothing like those achieved by the early railway trains which were capable of travelling at 60mph over a long distance. There were also major operating problems: steamers, road or rail, needed large regular quantities of coal and water to keep running, while some required a three man crew of driver, engineer and stoker. However, these features were not, in themselves, drawbacks which led to their development stagnating.

The road steamer pioneers were faced with a much more complex engineering design problem than their railway counterparts. They had to contend with steering difficulties of a kind never encountered before, in view of the weight and mass being moved. It is questionable whether any of the early engineers paid much attention, if any, to working out the centre of gravity of vehicles, especially in relation to the vehicle's dimensions, track, turning circle and cornering capabilities and speed; considerations that today would be regarded as a fundamental. Suspension systems had to be designed from scratch to provide even primitive ride qualities on the road surfaces which existed, although semi-elliptic steel springs had been used on coaches from mid-way through the eighteenth century. Engineers had to feel their way on chassis design and in fact it was not until the internal combustion engine came upon the scene that the French industry evolved the ladder form which eventually became an accepted part of the motor industry; 'chassis' is, of course, a French word. A totally new dimension on stopping vehicles

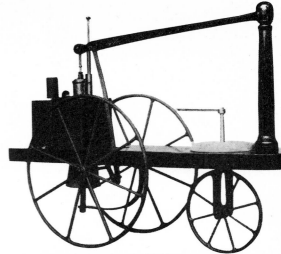

Above: The Frenchman Nicholas Cugnot is generally credited with producing the first road vehicle. Basically intended for hauling gun limbers, the design was transparently unstable with its boiler suspended ahead of the single driven axle

Right: A prolific inventor, Richard Trevithick built countless steam vehicle designs in the first decades of the nineteenth century, and his was the first truly successful road vehicle; he died in 1833

Left: William Murdoch of Redruth built this model steam engine in 1784. His attempts to develop a road vehicle from his experience with steam power for use in Cornish mines was largely frustrated by his employer, the famous James Watt. He produced this, however, so obviously a beam-engine on wheels

Far right: Richard Trevithick, who produced what was probably the most successful of the early steam driven vehicles in 1803

had to be evolved: braking technology had to be developed. Finally, some of the most important aspects of all: metallurgy was in its infancy as were precision tools able to manufacture components to anything like the tolerances required. In short, there had to be parallel development in design for all of the characteristics which now make up the modern mechanically propelled vehicle. The early road vehicle engineers bit off more than they could chew and had to wait for technical development in other spheres to catch up with steam engine design itself, which moved ahead at a faster rate comparatively than the other technologies primarily through railway and traction engine experience.

The 1890s were the years when the world's motor industry was truly born and the first load-carriers – trucks as we know them today – appeared. The centre of activity was still Europe with Germany and France joining Britain – and in several fields the engineers of those

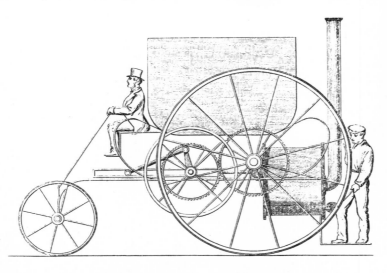

countries going ahead of the British – in development. Elsewhere in the world, only America pursued the same line. American urban developments in those days, generated straggly communities which were better suited to motor vehicles than horses. Unfortunately, the same rapid, thinly spread growth inevitably gave rise to roads that were ill-suited to anything faster or heavier than a trotting horse; hence, the market for auto-buggies developed in the early days rather than one for the ultra-heavy vehicles.

In the meantime, the Frenchman Leon Serpollet made a notable breakthrough in 1890 with his development of Ravel's idea of a petrol-powered steam wagon. Serpollet's design was most successful and was a major influence on subsequent road steam vehicle design. However, although petrol-fuelled steam engines were to become widely used, most makes persisted as solid fuel burners up to their demise.

Below left: the name of Foden was as well known in the late 19th century and early part of the 20th century for its steam wagon wagons as it is today for its diesel trucks. The company's steam-lorry interests originated, however, from experience producing traction engines. This particular design was evolved by Edwin Foden in the 1890s

England's restrictive legislation in the late 1890s did not entirely discourage the enterprise of its engineers; there was still plenty of scope, although mainly in the area of self-moving engines for agricultural use. It was in fact in 1880 that one of the main pioneers of commercial road vehicles in twentieth century Britain, Edwin Foden, first developed the highly successful two-cylinder steam engine design which was to give his company such a commanding position in road transport throughout much of the British Empire. Fodens, of Sandbach, Cheshire, were then making agricultural machinery, the company having started in this sphere in 1856. Many modern companies have agricultural machinery as their background, not least, of course, International Harvester which was already a world giant in this sphere in the 1890s. Quite a few companies who made their name in the steam wagon era accordingly made their debut as truck makers at this time; few, however, have survived the passing of the years.

The Lancashire Steam Motor Company Ltd, the forerunner of Leyland Motors, was founded in 1896. Like Fodens, it took national awards with its steam lorries and performed well in a series of important road trials for self-propelled vehicles in this period. Formed by Henry and George Spurrier and James Sumner, the Lancashire company succeeded in producing its first vehicle before the end of the year. This was a thirty hundredweight steam van with an oil-fired boiler and a two-cylinder compound engine which developed from 10 to 14hp. The drive was taken from spur gears on the crankshaft to a second motion shaft and thence by chain to a separate compensating shaft mechanism; chain final drive to the steel-tyred wheels was also used. It had three forward speeds and a reverse, all with separate friction clutches and levers. At trials at Manchester organised in 1897 for self-propelled vehicles by the Royal Agricultural Society of England, the vehicles obtained the highest award, a silver medal.

What was to be one of the most successful British truck making concerns, The Thornycroft Steam Wagon Co Ltd, was also founded in the 1890s. When this concern later switched to petrol and diesel driven trucks – it saw the way things were going in 1907 when it sold its steam

wagon rights and shifted to making petrol-engined trucks – it was equally successful until in 1961 it lost its separate identity in one of the company mergers that led to the modern British Leyland concern.

One of the 'firsts' in truck development was achieved in 1898 by Thornycroft; it built the first articulated outfit in the modern sense. This was a forward-control machine, and had a wooden cab with roof to protect the driver, and had its engine immediately behind the driver's seat.

While steam trucks were experiencing widespread development in Britain, the world's motor industry was being born and, even as the steam-engined commercial vehicle was moving into an era of economic acceptance, the first petrol-driven machines – to be followed by diesel-

powered units – were coming on the scene. There were to be three decades in which steam-driven commercial vehicles were manufactured side by side with the petrol and diesel-powered road vehicles and a further two decades of operation before steam was forced to give up the unequal struggle.

It is not difficult to see why the steam truck kept on so long in Britain (for they were being built right up to 1950): there was an abundance of cheap coal. In the USA, in contrast, in the sphere of commercial vehicles, the petrol-engined lorry killed the steamer stone dead almost before it was born. One reason was the ready availability of oil-based fuels, while another was the quite different labour market, unwilling to learn and practice the patient skills essential with steam vehicles. An exception was the New England-based White Manufacturing Company. Rollin White designed a very successful automotive steam engine in 1899 which led the company to start producing five ton steam trucks from

Above: by the 1900s, Thornycroft steamers were starting to look a little more like conventional trucks, although they were still rather crude in design

1900 onwards, continuing for a number of years until replaced by petrol-engined designs.

It is an interesting comparison that in 1925, when there were over twenty million petrol-driven vehicles on the roads of the USA, there were only just over one million petrol vehicles in Britain and substantially less numbers than that in every other European country where only France and Germany had sizeable vehicle parks. Until relatively recently, petrol-engined commercial vehicles dominated the commercial vehicle industry in America, and it was largely left to Europe to develop the diesel engine.

It was in 1876 that Nickolaus August Otto, at the engine factory he had established with Eugen Langen at Deutz in Germany, invented the four-stroke, spark ignition engine which bears his name. By creating the Otto engine, he established the principle of the 'Otto Cycle' (the

Above: Rudolf Diesel's original engine, built in 1898. This master unit is now in the Deutsche Museum in Munich

Right: this early Foden steamer represents the transitional design stage between tractor and truck

Left: Rudolf Diesel, who gave his name to the diesel engine, worked for a time for the German MAN company, who encouraged his work. Munich the location of MAN's present day headquarters for truck manufacture, also contains many of Diesel's early designs

Bottom: Gottlieb Daimler (right) and Wilhelm Maybach, his closest colleague in producing the first Daimler truck (second from right) with their first goods vehicle. Tiller steered, it employed the giant steel shod artillery wagon wheels which were a characteristic of many early truck designs

four-stroke principle) which was to be used subsequently in the great majority of petrol and compression-ignition engines. The location of Otto's factory at Deutz is also of interest for today it provides part of the name of one of Germany's leading truck manufacturers – Magirus Deutz – who are naturally proud of their distinguished founder.

The development of the truck in the last fifty years has, of course, gone hand in hand with the development of what is commonly, if somewhat misleadingly, known as the diesel engine. Surprisingly, perhaps, the automotive diesel owes very little to Rudolf Diesel's concepts. During the last two decades of the nineteenth century, work on oil-fuelled engines was being carried out by Priestman and Ackroyd Stuart in England and Diesel in Germany. Priestman was the first to make real progress, with a unit in which fuel was injected into the air charge in the cylinder while at maximum pressure – an essential feature of modern engines – and, indeed, Priestman made the first oil-engined lorry run in 1897. These engines still used an external ignition system, something Ackroyd Stuart overcame with his hot bulb principle. Diesel, meanwhile, was struggling to achieve automatic ignition by compressing the air to a high degree.

Daimler Benz lay claim to be the first commercial vehicle manufacturer to produce a range of trucks fitted with diesel engines in the 1920s, but this German company of course was also an early pioneer of petrol engines. In fact, Gottlieb Daimler's petrol engine developed in 1886 largely founded the era of the motor vehicle, and it was in September 1896, Daimler-Motoren-Gesellschaft (the forerunner of Daimler-Benz), supplemented the Daimler car with the first Daimler motor trucks. There were four models in the range offered with payloads from 1·5 to 5 tons, iron tyres and motors with power outputs from 4 to 10hp.

The initial success of his motor vehicles stimulated Gottlieb Daimler to make continual improvements to his motor truck. In 1898, an engine with Bosch magneto ignition was installed in a Daimler truck for the first time and it was the work of Robert Bosch and Frederick Simms in this and other fields which speeded the motor vehicle on its way. The invention tipped the balance in favour of the internal combustion engine against steam.

Whether the German company was the first producer of a purpose built goods vehicle is open to question, for two French manufacturers, Peugeot and Panhard, were – according to reports in the technical press of that time – offering proper delivery vans in 1895. It might, of course, be contended that, as the German vehicle had a greater payload, it was therefore a truck and not a car derived van. However, the French manufacturers, by creating light delivery vans almost from the word go, were undoubtedly the first to recognise the enormous potential market in the light delivery van which was really to mushroom in the early 1900s.

In the USA, meanwhile, the availability of oil in seemingly unlimited quantities meant that, although many inventors designed and built a steamer of two, few serious manufacturers tried to develop a steamer. There were exceptions, of course, as with White and, later, Baker. Zenon Hansen writing in *The Legend of the Bulldog*, the history of Mack Trucks, mentions in reference to Jack and Augustus Mack's early days in New York that, 'Legend has it that they produced an electric car and a steam-powered wagon, and that these vehicles were relegated to the nearby East River when their shortcomings became apparent'. He goes on to report that the first Mack motor vehicle, a twenty seater bus, was completed in 1900 after eight years of development. It had a four-cylinder engine, cone-type clutch, three-speed transmission and chain drive. Initially, it was used for eight years to carry sightseers through Brooklyn's Prospect Park, and then it was converted to a truck and retired after seventeen years and over one million miles of service. The success of *Old Number One* as it was known laid the foundation for the successful development of the Mack empire of today.

International Harvester by the 1890s had already carved its name wide in the agricultural markets of the world and somewhat naturally their move into the truck business came from a desire to produce vehicles to help the farmer. It was E. A. Johnston of the company's engineering department at the McCormick Works in Virginia who broke the ground, for he installed a petrol engine in a small truck and drove it between his home and the works for many months. Several years of development followed with the result that in 1905 he produced an Auto Buggy at International Harvester's Rock Fall Works; it was designed to look as much as possible like a horse drawn buggy. Like his original vehicle, the Auto Buggy was intended to carry a moderate amount of produce and allow the farmer to take his family to church on Sundays. Powered by a two-cylinder, air-cooled engine, both the Auto Buggy and the Auto Wagon, which immediately followed it when production was started in 1907, were fitted with large cart type wheels which gave good clearance over rough ground; one imagines it did not do much for the comfort of the driver. Such was the success of these machines that they were put into full production at Akron, Ohio, at the company's first truck plant.

Who actually built the first motor truck in the USA is open to question. In manufacturing terms, Ford appears to have done so in 1899 with the sale of a panel delivery vehicle to a shoe company in Detroit. Many of Ford's model A vehicles were, however, converted from car to goods vehicle use.

That it was the horse and not the steamer which was still regarded as the main competition of the early automotive truck producer – particularly in the USA – is revealed in the Ford literature of that period: 'It doesn't need feeding when standing still' was the slogan for the model T Ford even after World War I. The original Model T was available as a delivery van and a light pickup for country estates. For the first time, many businesses could afford motor transport, since the Model T cost half as much to run as a horse and cart.

Apart from producing the first steam-powered and petrol engine trucks, the 1890s also saw considerable experimenting with electric vans which made use of storage batteries as the power source. It was recognised that they had no future in the heavy vehicle sector, but possessed distinct possibilities in low payload, city delivery applications. Naturally, their range was limited, but even then journeys of up to one hundred miles were accomplished on a single charge; thirty to forty miles was, however, the more normal economic range. The major problem, recognised from the outset and still true today, was the weight of the vehicle in relation to its payload. At this time, one of the biggest headaches for the electric vehicle manufacturer was found to be the damage caused to the battery from the jolting of the vehicle over poorly surfaced streets on its solid tyres. As a result, the designers gave particular attention to strengthening the design of the accumulator to withstand rough treatment and improving the suspension of the battery itself on the vehicle to counter the affect of shocks transmitted from uneven road surfaces; many electric vehicles had to be withdrawn from use because of vibration damage. Operating cost was measured in terms of watt/hours per ton per mile run, but the high weight, laden or unladen, meant one of the biggest cost elements was found to be on tyres. Naturally, however, in spite of the operating problems encountered, those who favoured electric vehicles expounded their environmental virtues: that they left no dirt, gas, smoke or smell behind them.

The battering which trucks got led to a widespread search for tyre improvements. The British Dunlop company and the French Michelin concern were the pioneers. It is reported that in 1902 Dunlop in London

Below: International Harvester's origins as a truck manufacturer go back to the early 1900s when they ventured into the Auto Buggy market. Designed to look like a horse-drawn buggy, it was essentially a dual purpose vehicle, built for farmers to carry both their families and farm produce

Top: John Boyd Dunlop, whose pneumatic tyres for bicycles and cars were eventually adapted to truck use in quantity in the 1920s. The picture above shows a replica of Dunlop's first experimental pneumatic tyre, which consisted of an inflated sheet of rubber tube covered with canvas and fixed to a wooden disc

Right: one of the first Swedish trucks, if not the first, was this Vabis machine, built in 1903. Vabis later linked with Scania to form Scania-Vabis. The Vabis name largely disappeared on the relatively recent formation of Saab-Scania

purchased a Daimler truck and equipped it with pneumatic tyres. That was the beginning of pneumatic tyres for commercial vehicles although the first pneumatic tyre specially for trucks was not to be manufactured until 1912 by Michelin who had produced numerous special tyres by then including balloon tyres (low profile fat singles) for desert use in 1896.

One of the outstanding features of the 1890s and early 1900s was the number of avenues explored in the course of developing the ultimate in mechanically propelled road vehicles. Take fuel, for example. An incredible variety of different gases and liquid fuels were tried: apart from coal and coke in steam wagons, paraffin, benzol and alcohol were the rivals to petrol; wood alcohol – surprisingly, perhaps – had a particularly strong following for a while, notably in France. Producer gas, another long-standing delight for experimenters if not for the drivers of vehicles thus powered, was with us then and is with us still. Obviously, all these fuels had merits as well as disadvantages, but the overriding consideration which led to them not catching on was that they could not be produced in sufficient quantities for commercial use.

Part of the background to this situation was that there was a world oil crisis! Almost as soon as the USA started building cars and trucks, the country's domestic demand for oil for automotive and industrial purposes rocketed and the US Government reduced drastically its oil exports. This left Europe searching for alternative producers; British interests, for example, were looking at this time to Sumatra, Borneo and Rumania as sources of supply. Already in Europe there was, moreover, a preoccupation with fuel availability in the event of war as European countries realised just how dependent their embryo motor industries were on imported fuels.

The experiments were not confined to fuel. Numerous ideas were tried for every component from starters to transmissions. Before the electric starter was accepted for trucks, hand-cranking was the norm, but obviously with heavier truck engines this was quite a job. Starting by firing cartridges was considered very seriously and in fact the English Wolseley concern developed a big 140bhp six-cylinder engine for use in the USA in which cordite cartridges were used to fire the first three cylinders in the firing cycle with the ordinary electric ignition operating on the other three with the conventional ignition then taking over completely.

Views on transmissions varied almost as much as those on the steam versus petrol argument. Whatever the system selected by the manufacturer, it was criticised. Some favoured Panhard's sliding tooth type, others the De Dion system where the gears were always in mesh and used with expanding friction clutches. Designers were, of course, finding very different problems with trucks than with private cars arising from the former's need for a greater gear reduction requirement. By the end of the 1900s, the constant mesh or planetary gearbox of the type developed by Lanchester was vying with sliding mesh designs for the lead in use on commercial vehicles.

In 1905, Commercial Cars Ltd, now part of the Chrysler Corporation, had built its first truck and fitted it with the Linley pre-selector gearbox, a development which was to have an influence on truck gearbox design in the years to come, although not perhaps as much as the Wilson gearbox which had yet to appear.

Automatic transmissions were also born in the 1900s through the work of a German, Dr H. Föttinger. His original patents were developed in Britain with Leyland achieving the greatest advances in their commercial vehicle designs. It is also true to say that American automatic transmissions have developed from Föttinger's principles.

There were soon to be conflicting views on the drive arrangement from the gearbox to the back axle. There were those who maintained that there was no better answer than a chain drive and that, while a propeller shaft and differential might be suitable for cars, it was certainly not right for trucks. As it happened, of course, on the car-derived, petrol-powered goods vehicles of the lighter type, the propeller shaft with universal joint and differential rear axle was applied increasingly in the 1900s. In contrast, on heavier outfits (1½ tons payload and above) chain drive was generally the accepted method and remained so on some machines right up to the 1930s. Propeller shafts on many makes of truck did not really take over until the 1920s and even in 1925 there were many firms offering the option.

One of the pioneers of the propeller shaft drive on trucks was Dennis Brothers of Guildford, who fitted 'worm driving gear and driving axle connections', as they termed them, in 1904. They also sold the idea for use on Milnes-Daimlers. Unfortunately, numerous breakdowns at first checked development but Dennis persisted with the concept and, by development, eventually got things right. There were, of course, many variations on the drive theme, including separate propeller shafts to each rear axle.

The French Latil truck produced in 1906 was one of the first successful front wheel drive goods vehicles. Based on an earlier private car front wheel drive design, this Latil model was built at the Suresnes factory which is now a main plant of Saviem, Renault's truck-making concern, which acquired Latil in 1955. There were, too, designs where the drive was through an electric generator. A good example is that of the vehicles produced for use in New York by the Fischer Company. In this instance, instead of the power from the engine being transmitted direct to the

drive axle, it was used to drive an electric generator which in turn drove two electric motors geared directly to the vehicle's wheels. This was a concept used a few years later in England on the petrol-electric vehicles built successfully by the Tilling Stevens concern of Maidstone.

Development of the oil engine in the 1900s was not confined to Diesel's activities. In fact, oil engines produced in this period by Ruston and Hornsby-Akroyd were very much more successful than Diesel's, but not applied to automotive duties. It was fuel injection which gave Diesel his biggest problem for he persisted with his air-blast system. The jerk-type fuel injection pump had not yet arrived on the scene, although a mechanical fuel pump was in fact fitted from the outset in the 1900s on Hornsby-Akroyd and Ruston engines, the design of which incidentally was much closer to that of the present day compression-ignition engine than Diesel's own designs.

In terms of component development, one of the Swedish industry's most valuable contributions to the advancement of truck design occurred in 1909 when a Scania truck fitted with wheels running on ball bearings successfully completed a record-breaking trip from Malmo to Stockholm. Sven Winquist, the inventor of the ball bearing, went along on the trip. Since then, of course, Sweden has become world famous for its high quality steel bearings of all kinds.

Hot tube, coil and battery ignition systems which had been the norm in the early vehicles were gradually superseded by the magneto developed by the Englishman Simms and the German Bosch. Simms, of course, had his finger in all different kinds of pies, from armoured cars to airships. Some of his more mundane but off-beat ideas detailed by Bryan Morgan in his excellent story of Simms were for a bumper with cushioning properties and another bumper which 'stuck out like a cats whiskers to push open the garage doors'.

Comparative performances of different concepts in trucks was monitored closely, hence the tremendous interest in the vehicle trials of this period, conducted mainly in England, France and Germany, when detailed appraisals were made of speeds, fuel consumptions, carrying capacities, gradient performance and reliability. Speeds of up to 10mph on these trials (average 8mph) were normal at this time for trucks carrying 3–4 tons payload and fuel consumption which varied widely from 5 to 12mpg on petrol-powered vehicles. These trials could be exhausting affairs. In Britain, the Royal Automobile Club held trials of 1000 miles for commercial vehicles which lasted 22 days involving 19 petrol-powered 3 ton vehicles and 10 petrol and steam-powered 5 ton wagons. One of the 3 tonners achieved a fuel consumption of 9mpg over 927 miles. In the USA, testing (with exceptions) tended to be of a more individual type as opposed to mass trials. For example, the technical press of the day reported the results of rigorous tests on a Packard Truck in the White Mountains which ended with an ascent of Mount Washington, the highest point in eastern America. This two-cylinder engined 15bhp vehicle is reported to have achieved a fuel consumption of 11mpg on its journey while carrying a load of 2000 lb initially and increasing to 3200 lb shortly after its start. Its three-forward-speed gearbox permitted it to negotiate gradients up to 1 in 4.6.

Few petrol powered goods vehicles in the early 1900s were designed to carry more than 3 tons – in fact there were serious doubts whether even a 5 tonner was feasible – but the first of the many uplifts in weights was soon to come. By the end of the decade, there were load carriers with a capacity of 7 to 8 tons to be found – mainly steamers, of course, but some petrol designs. In fact, Leyland who were producing both steam and petrol vehicles commented that, below 4 tons, economics favoured the petrol vehicle; over 6 tons the steamer. The high costs of petrol and rubber tyres were the reasons given for this situation.

Top: this 1902 Rapid truck was called a 'one lunger' because of its single cylinder engine. Designed by Max Grabowsky, it had a chain drive and the steering column was on the right

Above: the first truck to carry the GMC emblem was this forward control, or cab-over-engine, four-wheeler, built in 1908

Above right: an early advertisement for Foden steam wagons by a prominent London main dealer emphasised availability of spares and after-sales-service facilities

Right: Sentinel steamers could be seen on British roads right up to the 1950s. In the 1920s, Sentinel was the clear market leader in the UK, manufacturing at the company's plant in Shrewsbury. It was, however, by Alley and Maclellan of Glasgow that this Sentinel steamer was produced in 1905

Handbuilding was the order of the day, of course, and it is appropriate
– since it sums up the age admirably – to record the reminiscence of the
1900s of Mr Max Grabowsky of GMC which was reported in his firm's
Truck News of 1946 as follows: 'We had to start from scratch. We used
structural steel and tested it ourselved, designed, forged and machined
every part of the vehicle in our own shop'.

Only a handful of companies worldwide had produced more than the
occasional truck by 1900, but the floodgates were shortly to open.
Many of today's American and European giants have their origins in
the years following the turn of the century. Europe led in all sectors at
this stage, but the decade saw not only the birth of the American truck
industry but the formation of its structure, which was to make it the
world leader in volume production terms, although not in design,
through the adoption at an early stage of production line techniques.

The early success that the German manufacturers experienced in the
1890s continued into the 1900s with Daimler, Maybach and Benz
patents finding their way all over the world. The US motor industry
benefited remarkably from the Daimler and Benz designs largely through
the work of William Steinway, the piano manufacturer, who owned the
American Daimler Company. Daimler vehicles manufactured in the
USA are reported to have attracted considerable interest at the New
York Automobile Exhibition of 1900. The American Daimler Company

achieved what may well have been a world first the following year when it set up in Philadelphia an after-sales and tow-in service.

Apart from Daimler-Benz, there is in fact only one survivor of the pioneer German concerns which produced their first truck shortly after the turn of the century. This is the firm of FAUN (Fahrzeugfabrik Ansbäch and Nürnburg) which today specialises in custom-built heavy haulage vehicles, dump trucks and carriers for lorry mounted mobile cranes.

Although what is now Germany's second largest manufacturer, MAN, was not building trucks in the 1900s, one of their acquisitions of the 1960s – the Büssing concern – was making them in some quantity, having produced the first in 1901. At that time, Germany itself was not a fruitful field for commercial vehicle sales. Companies like Daimler-Benz, Büssing and Dürkopp of Bielefeld (one of several then substantial German manufacturers no longer in business) had their biggest early successes in England. In fact, when the Daimler and Benz vehicles proved themselves in England, there was greater acceptance in the truck market of Germany.

The 1900s saw the formation of the first of the main parts of today's Chrysler Corporation to build trucks. This was Commercial Cars Ltd, founded at Lavender Hill London in 1905, by a group of enthusiasts carrying out experiments with the Linley gearbox, a pre-selector unit with a change-speed lever on the steering column. The company's first truck, a four-ton vehicle with iron tyres and upright steering, came off the production line in that year. It was twelve months later that Commercial Cars moved to Luton where the company started to build three tonners with four-cylinder 30hp T-head petrol engines and chain drive, and it was with these models that Commer, as they were now known, first established its reputation for workmanship by winning a silver medal in one of the first reliability trials. As part of the Rootes Group, the Company was acquired by Chrysler in 1964.

Of all the firms that have been welded together to form the Truck and Bus Division of British Leyland, one company stands head and shoulders above the rest. This is Associated Commercial Vehicles. When acquired by Leyland in the 1960s, ACV itself comprised not only AEC (the Associated Equipment Company, which had its origins in a Walthamstow bus repair works in the 1900s), but Crossley, Maudslay, Park Royal, Charles H. Roe and Transport Equipment (Thornycroft).

In 1909, AEC received its rather obscure name and in 1910 produced its first master piece, the world-famous B-type double deck bus. Most went to the London General Omnibus Company (which was the concern associated with AEC), and the firm was to be thought of primarily as a bus producer thereafter. In fact, this was not accurate because AEC in the next fifty years was to produce some highly successful trucks. The first of these was the Y series four-tonner, a robust vehicle fitted with a 45hp petrol engine and four-speed gearbox and which had a very distinguished service in World War I.

One of the most significant of the ACV companies was Maudslay which in 1905 produced for that time a very advanced truck design. The model concerned was a five-tonner powered by a three-cylinder 27hp engine which, unusually at that time, drove through a four-speed gearbox and a propeller shaft. A second company formed in 1912 which built up a formidable reputation for its buses in subsequent years was the Bristol Tramways and Carriage Co Ltd. Like AEC, Bristol also produced a four-ton truck soon after its formation, and they continued in the lorry business right up to the late 1960s when production was gradually phased out.

Another famous British company – Guy Motors – was founded in 1914 shortly before World War I. Sydney Guy, who until then had been

A pre-World War I Federal truck carrying a boiler in the Sierra foothills, east of Madeira, California. The vehicle was operated by the Madeira Sugar Pine Lumber Co

34

works manager of the Sunbeam Motor Co, built the company's first truck (a 1½-tonner) which incorporated a number of original ideas. Instead of the heavy rolled-steel channel frames commonly used at that time, he also employed a much lighter form of pressed-steel frame. He also introduced a three-point flexible suspension to prevent distortion from being transmitted to the engine and gearbox. Yet a third unusual feature was the fitment of direct drive in third gear for use when fully laden, while the indirect top gear was used only when travelling lightly. Guy enthusiasts point out that in later years this was also looked on as original in some quarters and known as 'overdrive'. Guy was first acquired by the Jaguar car concern in the 1960s and is now part of British Leyland.

With the French manufacturers, the names of De Dion Bouton, Panhard and Peugeot are synonymous with the birth of the motor

industry. Of these, only Peugeot remains, but in commercial vehicle terms only as a light van producer. The names of the companies which are left all commenced commercial vehicle manufacturere in the 1900s – Berliot, Renault and Unic; Unic is now the French offshoot of Fiat.

Berliet was founded in the 1890s by Marius Berliet as a car manufacturing concern and the first commercial vehicles produced in the 1900s were based on the car chassis. A feature of all these models was that they were forward control designs and fitted some of the biggest engines of that time, producing up to 80bhp. Many manufacturers, particularly the French ones, were producing vehicles of the forward control (cab over engine) configuration. So, when Peugeot produced a normal control, bonneted model in 1906, it was out of the conventional run of things.

Renault, which now produces trucks under the name of Saviem, built its first truck – a 10hp delivery van – in 1906 and a range of goods carriers of up to five tons payload quickly followed. Unic were also founded in 1906, and started life (and remained) a light van producer.

In the 1900s, however, De Dion Bouton, Panhard and Latil were the key companies in the French industry. The contribution of Latil (who started production in 1906 and who were to be absorbed into the Saviem Group in 1955) was particularly notable for it designed a four-wheel-drive tractor unit which was to be particularly successful for hauling guns and other heavy loads in World War 1. The design eventually established Latil as a main producer of tractor units for articulated vehicle work. De Dion Bouton moved successfully into municipal vehicles with a low frame chassis design intended specifically for refuse collecting.

It was in 1903 that the first Italian truck appeared. This 24hp vehicle, a Fiat, had a two-piece block four-cylinder petrol engine placed ahead of the front axle under the driver's seat. It had a simple loading platform/body, four metres long and two metres wide; it could reach a speed of 13kph (8mph) with a payload of four tons. The gearbox, in the middle of the chassis, was connected to the engine by means of a propeller shaft, and by chains to the wheels, which were of the wood spoke artillery type.

In 1904, one of these trucks made a demonstration journey (Turin-Genoa-Nice and back) with a load of 33 tons at an average speed of more than 10khp (6mph) without any trouble.

Of the companies now welded into the Fiat Group, Lancia, OM and SPA all were formed in the years before the World War I. Vincenzo Lancia, who founded the company which bears his name in 1907, did not start truck production until the war, but his company continues to produce various models right up to the present day.

The Brescia-based firm of OM was formed in 1906 as Brixia-Züst and built its first truck two years later. Acquired in 1918 by Societa Anonima Officine Meccaniche, the name OM was adopted and has been used ever since; it is still used on some lighter Fiat models by whom it was acquired in the 1960s. Although at the present time Fiat stands supreme in Italy, in the early days of the century there were quite a few competitors. Most of them are now part of Fiat, but an exception was Isotta-Fraschini, formed by Cesare Isotta and Oreste Fraschini, better known perhaps for their private cars. This company started producing trucks soon after its formation in 1904, continuing with bread-and-butter designs right up to the late 1940s.

Another company, Bianchi, formed by bicycle manufacturer Edoardo Bianchi of Milan, who founded his business in 1912, was in a rather different category. Although in the early days most of the trucks produced were of a conventional design, the company introduced a number of interesting innovations before ceasing production in the late 1950s. SPA has formed part of Fiat for over fifty years, the company having been acquired by the Italian giant in 1927. It was founded in 1906 by Michele Ansaldi and Mateo Ceirano, starting truck manufacture almost immediately. Large numbers of trucks were built during World War I, and it was in the post-war years that financial difficulties lead to take over. The name, however, continued right up to the late 1940s.

In the 1900s, the Austro-Hungarian Empire was still a major power in Europe, and it is therefore appropriate to remember that the factories of the main producers of that time, including Austro-Daimler, Graf and Stift (which built its first trucks – for the Austrian army – in 1910), OAF (formed in 1907 as Osterreichische Autobolfabriks AG, again building mainly army trucks) and Saurer Osterreich (founded 1906), played a much more important role in the scheme of things than they do today. The break up of the Hapsburg Empire also meant the demise in any significant terms of an Austrian motor industry. A major legacy left is, of course, the Czechoslovakian industry, the present Czech manufacturing companies of Skoda, Tatra and Praga all having their origins in the 1890s and 1900s when Czechoslovakia as we know it today formed part of the Austro-Hungarian Empire.

Skoda was originally a motor cycle manufacturer in the 1890s using the name Laurin und Klement, and did not start truck production until the 1900s. It was a very successful truck producer and in 1925 was absorbed by the giant Skoda organisation. Tatra's origins are even older than those of Skoda, its interest in truck manufacture having arisen out of fifty years of engineering experience. That was in 1900 when Nesselsdorfer Wagenfabrik as the company was then known produced its first truck; the name Tatra was adopted just after the World War I. The youngest of the Czech producers, Praga Motor Works as it was originally named, was founded in 1907, building its first models to the Italian Isotta Fraschini design and then to its own formula.

In the rest of the Austro-Hungarian Empire, the only significant development seems to have been in Hungary by the Ikarus concern in 1913, but with buses not trucks, and the RABA (Hungarian Railway Carriage and Machine Works) in Gyor which produced a variety of vehicles. Mention of the Saurer in the Austrian context, of course,

Below: a 7-ton coal wagon built by the Four Wheel Drive Wagon Co of Milwaukee, Wisconsin

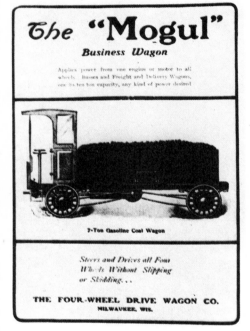

38

Below: after early development of its steamers, Leyland moved into petrol-engined vehicle production. The company produced both these vehicles in 1914; the top one was a 4-tonner general haulage model operated by a Liverpool sugar refinery and the bottom one a purpose-built outfit, also with a 4-ton payload

makes it appropriate to recall the work of Adolf Saurer who first started building petrol engines in his own Switzerland in 1888, and who in 1903 built his first truck, a 5-ton unit. The engine fitted in this vehicle had the distinction of being fitted with the first ever rudimentary turbocharger to improve its breathing. Saurer, of course, was also responsible for creating the first automotive diesel engine which, produced in 1908 with Diesel's help, consisted of a Safir four-cylinder petrol engine converted to oil burning.

Saurer's contribution to early truck design was very significant. Not only were Saurer vehicles exported to many overseas countries, but the company's engine and other design patents were so extensive and practical that they were adopted by many foreign manufacturers including companies in Britain and the USA. Later, in fact, an agreement with Britain's Armstrong-Whitworth led to the production for

some years in Britain of the Armstrong Saurer heavy duty truck. A point of interest is that Saurer produced an engine brake in the 1900s. As in modern engine brake designs, by compressing the air in the engine, it turned the power unit into a retarder. As a company, Saurer still exerts a profound influence on European diesel engine design and in fact the latest units of one major European Group are virtually Saurer designed.

British interest in Swiss designs was also apparent with a second concern, Berna (first Berna Motorwagenfabrik and later Motorwagenfabrik Berna). This company started building trucks in 1906, and for a while shortly afterwards was owned by British interests. Although it returned to Swiss hands, links with Britain were reflected for many years as it was a make which was to sell strongly in the UK well into the 1920s. Saurer, Berna and a third Swiss manufacturer, FBW, standing for Franz Brozincevic and Co and founded in 1904, are still going strong today, although their combined truck production is no more than 1000 annually.

Of the petrol-engined vehicles produced in the 1900s, many were of the dual-purpose type in that some were specifically designed so that the passenger carrying body could be lifted off and a goods body substituted; others were passenger and goods carriers. The Swedish industry started off in this way with the Scania concern (still alive today as Saab-Scania of Sodertalje) being the first mass producer of vehicles in Scandinavia. Scania's first vehicle built in 1903, for instance, was designed as an estate car or station wagon: the body was divided up so that the rear section, which included the passenger compartment, could be removed and replaced by a body for goods carrying. The original buyer of this vehicle, a Mr Bjurling, was engaged in manufacturing as well as import and export of pharmaceuticals, so he therefore used the vehicle for both passenger and goods transport.

The first Scania model was really quite advanced in several ways. The lubricating system, for instance, was designed around a lubricator, a bronze container with level sight glass mounted on the bulkhead behind the steering wheel. Using a separate hand pump, the driver pumped lubricating oil to the engine big-end bearings every now and then. Other lubrication points, such as the main bearings, camshaft bearings and drive shaft bearings, were supplied with lubricating oil automatically via an adjustable drip valve system on the lubricator. The engine itself was of a conventional type, for it had two cylinders and developed 8hp at 800rpm. During the first few years, Scania imported engines from Kemper Motorenfabrik in Berlin – unlike the other early Swedish pioneer, Vabis in Sodertalje, which manufactured its own engines right from 1897 when it built its first private car. Vabis, which was to link up with Scania soon after producing its first truck in 1903, formed the nucleus of what is today one of the strongest truck producing combines in the world.

Strangely, perhaps, Russia had no truck industry of any kind, relying on imports from Germany, Austria, France and England, and this was a situation which was to continue right through to the 1920s.

In the USA in the 1900s, vehicle manufacture was moving ahead fast. Already the giants of the 1970s were staking their claims to the future, with the founders of the present GMC and Chrysler empires following hot on the heels of Ford and International Harvester. Two Detroit companies, the Rapid Motor Vehicle Company and the Reliance Motor Company, provided the basis of the GMC Truck and Coach Division. A little single-cylinder truck produced in 1900 was the first true baby of the giant GMC. Designed by Max Grabowsky it had a horizontal engine, was chain driven and, as a result of its sale to a garment cleaners in Detroit, the Rapid company was formed. It was in fact the cleaners – the American Garment Cleaning Company – who invested in the company which, during the first three years of its existence, built and sold 75 trucks. However, as he needed more space and finance, Grabowsky made a deal with another vehicle manufacturer, the Pontiac Spring and Wagon Works, to invest money and to take over production. As a result, a plant was built at Pontiac in 1905 and Rapid moved in. In 1906, Rapid built two hundred trucks of about twenty different types, and over the next three years manufacturing facilities were enlarged to deal with demand until in 1909, Rapid joined General Motors.

The Reliance Motor Company started in business in Detroit in 1902 as a passenger car and truck manufacturer, and in 1907 a 3-ton Reliance, using a twin-cylinder engine equipped with a special gearless friction transmission, made a spectacular winter run from Detroit to Chicago. A distance of 304 miles was covered in less than four days, and it proved a stunt which helped attract attention to the mid-winter Chicago Motor Show. Then, late in 1908 Reliance was purchased by GMC and, like the Rapid, its product name was officially changed to GMC in 1913. The initials GMC were first used on trucks in 1911 in the business of the General Motors Truck Company. Both petrol and electric commercial vehicles were shown by this company at the New York Madison Square Garden Auto Show in 1912, under the GMC trade name. The petrol models were in the 1, 2 and 3-ton category, built at the Rapid plant in Pontiac, while the electric in 1, 1/2, 3 and 6-ton sizes had been built at the Reliance plant at Owosso, Michigan. Truck manufacturing operations were, however, consolidated at the Pontiac plant in 1913.

The present Chrysler Corporation is a complex welding of famous vehicle makers worldwide. Dodge is, however, its most famous name,

Below: the distinctive appearance of the 1913 International owed much to the neat bonnet. The bonnet cover when removed gave good access to the 40hp engine (see detail picture)

Below: powered by a 12bhp single-cylinder engine located under the seat, this Reo truck built towards the end of the 1900s owed a lot to the traditional carriage builder's craft. It employed chain drive (see detail picture) and featured wooden spoked wheels

although the two Dodge brothers, who started in business in 1899 making bicycles, did not actually start vehicle manufacture until 1914. John and Horace Dodge, founders of the automobile manufacturing company in 1914, left their birthplace, Niles, Michigan, in 1899 to move to Windsor, Ontario, to manufacture bicycles under the name Evans and Dodge. In 1901, the brothers moved to Detroit to become automobile part makers producing axles, transmissions, steering gears and crankcases in ever increasing quantities. Then in 1910 the purchase of the present site of the Dodge Assembly Plant in Hamtramck, Michigan, established Dodge Brothers as the largest automotive parts organisation in the country; by 1914, the firm had built parts for more than 500,000 cars. When the brothers decided to build a car bearing their own name in 1914, more than 22,000 firms applied for dealerships. On 14 November of that year, the first Dodge car was unveiled, a four-cylinder vehicle which weighed 2000lb, was 6ft 9in high and 13ft long. Truck manufacture was soon to follow.

Ford built the foundation of its later success in the light truck business in the years before World War I. Its first delivery vehicle, the model E, introduced in 1904 was replaced in 1911 by the Model T powered by a 20hp engine and which was produced as a 7½cwt and 1-tonner.

Autocar, Diamond T, Reo, FWD and Hendrickson were among the world's other well known names to start in the truck business in the 1900s. The year 1907 saw the first Autocar truck, a short wheelbase 2-tonner. Such was the success of this vehicle, that huge quantities were sold, and the result was that in 1910 this concern decided to abandon car production which it had begun in 1899. Autocar is now part of the White Motor Corporation.

Another company which is now also part of White is Diamond T, which owes its name to the fact that the father of the founder, Charles Tilt, ran a shoe manufacturing business, the trade mark of which was a diamond. Then, when the son started building cars in 1905, it was under the name of the Diamond T Motor Co, the T, of course, standing for Tilt. The first Diamond T truck was produced in 1911 from the company's plant in Chicago.

A third company now part of White Motor Corporation is that of Reo, a name stemming from the initials of R.E. Old, of Oldsmobile fame. He, along with a group of other businessmen, founded Reo in Lansing, Michigan, in 1904 to produce first cars and then in 1908 trucks and buses. The first truck was a light delivery model, and what is believed to be a 'first' was secured in 1910 with a model fitted as standard with pneumatic tyres.

The names Autocar, Diamond T and Reo are still much in evidence today, but one name worthy of mention which has also been absorbed by White – at the beginning of the 1950s – is that of Sterling. Sterlings were originally called Sternbergs in 1907, the name being changed in 1914. It was a name which, like the others now in the White Corporation, was to become particularly significant in the two world wars.

The initials FWD, predictably perhaps, stands for Four Wheel Drive, a concept which two Wisconsin blacksmiths, Otto Zachow and William Besserdich, relied on from the start when they founded their business at Clintonville in 1908. Applied first in a private car, the concept was almost immediately applied to a 2-ton truck. From there, the company never looked back, especially when the merits of the principle were appreciated in the conditions of World War I.

Magnus Hendrickson was yet one more of the many pioneers who translated bicycle making skills to trucks, for he built his first in 1900. It was not until 1913, however, that he formed the Hendrickson Motor Truck Company in Chicago, specialising in the custom-built product for which the company is still well known today. There were, of course, many other manufacturers which met with varying degrees of success over this period. Some lasted for two or three decades and it is appropriate to pick out the names of two or three of them, of which one made a particularly big contribution to truck development, while the stories of the other two reflect what was to happen to most of the other commercial vehicle manufacturers.

The company which made the outstanding contribution was the Packard Motor Company formed in 1899. When the first truck was to run coast to coast across the USA in 1912, it was a Packard, reflecting the fact that the company was then the number one in volume truck production in the USA and possibly worldwide. The 3-ton truck completed the journey in 46 days, which was no mean feat at that time. After a distinguished contribution in World War I, the Packard truck was, however, phased out in the 1920s in favour of quality car production.

So to the two companies whose record is typical of what happened to so many truck producers. The Selden Motor Vehicle Company of Rochester, New York, started making trucks in 1912 and sold them on the then unusual system of hire purchase. Like Packard, efforts were aided by war contracts, but excessive national production coupled with lack of success with post-war designs led to the company's closure. 'The acme of engineering perfection', was how the American-built Pierce Arrows were described when offered on the British Market. Founded in 1911 in Boston, Massachusetts, the company was wedded from the start to propeller-shaft drive, and its 2 and 5-ton models met with immediate success. After a World War I boom, the company, like Sterling, slipped downhill before closing its doors finally around 1927 for just the same reasons.

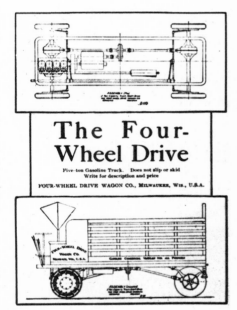

CHAPTER 2

Wagons at War

When World War I broke out in August 1914, there was an immediate demand for motor vehicles from all the countries involved in the hostilities. They needed vehicles for every purpose, from troop carrying and supplies movement to gun and munitions hauling. However, as soon as they reached the theatres of war, many kinds of unforeseen problems were encountered. The conditions imposed by war threw up design weaknesses right from the start; inadequate power-to-weight ratios, insufficient ground clearance and inadequate protection against the ingress of water and mud were just a few of them. If a truck became bogged down, it often had to be manhandled clear. Wheels spinning in the mud led to tyres coming loose from the rims which whizzed round inside the covers causing them to lozenge and come adrift altogether. Underpowered vehicles led to snail's pace movement of convoys. Inadequate ground clearance not only led to vehicles grounding but also to immediate damage to main driveline components; moisture finding its way into plugs, wiring and magnetos was a constant 'stopper'.

Steam wagons, seemingly ideal for carrying heavy loads and for gun hauling, ran into particular difficulties (largely through their weight) in the deep mud of Flanders, although this was less of a problem where tracks were fitted as they tended to spread the weight.

The forward areas, of course, provided manufacturers with an excellent proving ground for their products. Cut up by shell fire and churned up by men, animals and equipment, such terrain offered the worst possible operating conditions. Their severity could never have been simulated on a test circuit – even had there been such a thing at the time.

Probably the most far reaching impact of the war on the world's embryonic truck industry was the realisation of the value of the truck for moving troops and supplies from railheads to battle areas. Here, the virtues of the lighter, more versatile, petrol-engined machine were immediately apparent and swung the balance in its favour against the heavy, less manoeuvrable steamer.

Fortunately for the British, pre-war trials had shown that for military purposes the self-contained load carrier was preferable to the steam traction engine which, in military terms, was regarded primarily as a hauling vehicle. Nevertheless, steam was to play its part in quite a big way, certainly in the early days of the war. Around 1000 Foden steam trucks alone were supplied for military use in this period and most of the other steam truck producers were represented in France. A great many of the trucks (both petrol and steam powered) which were delivered to the Allies were used on the Western and the Italian-Austrian fronts;

When Leyland went to war in 1914, the company's activities were not confined to truck production. Here in this 1915 photograph, armoured cars await despatch to the front

they were also used further afield, in limited quantities, against the Turks in the Middle East – in what were then Mesopotamia and Palestine – and on the Russian front, at least in the early days of the war. In fact, the Russian army was supplied with several thousand vehicles by British and American manufacturers, notably Foden, Garrett, Fowler, AEC, Star, Austin, Caledon, Napier and Burford from Great Britain and Packard, White, FWD and Garford from the USA. It was not, however, until the war started that the strategic significance of trucks became strongly apparent to everyone. Immediately, the supply of certain component parts made only in Germany dried up for the opposing nations. Similarly, items manufactured principally in France and Britain ceased to be available to Germany and the Austro-Hungarian Empire. There were lessons which, in the post-war years, taught the main world powers to follow the road of self-sufficiency in truck production.

In Britain, despite vociferous warnings from the industry's leaders about the truck industry's dependence on German component supplies, there was an immediate problem over the supply of magnetos – the production of which was largely in the hands of the German Bosch concern. In the same way, the Germans were hit by a tyre shortage precipitated because the British Dunlop and French Michelin concerns were their main suppliers. To illustrate what happened over component supply, it is worth taking magnetos as an example. In Britain, Simms Magnetos Ltd started producing units to its own design in 1907, having relinquished its association with Bosch on the formation of the company. Very high quality units were produced, and companies to make magnetos from Simms' designs were soon established in France and the USA. However, the company found that recruiting labour with the requisite skills was difficult and this, along with slow market conditions, resulted in the British company closing down its plant, the staff being taken over by the British Thomson Houston Company, which was also making magnetos.

With war approaching fast, this left the country in a vulnerable state as Bosch reverted to their position as the main suppliers. The late St John Nixon, writing in *The Simms Story*, conjures up the scene very clearly. He writes: 'Before the First World War broke out, the War Office, the Admiralty and numbers of British car manufacturers, who were relying on foreign made magnetos, were warned repeatedly of the serious situation that would arise if this country were involved in a war without there being any British-made magnetos available in large quantities. The warning went unheeded, and as the Government gave the Simms Magneto Company Ltd very feeble support, in spite of high quality work being turned out, the Company in its then existing form was forced to close down, some eighteen months before the outbreak of the war, but Simms Motor Units Ltd was formed in April, 1913, to take its place. Thus, Simms' well intended affort to establish a magneto industry in this country and so render England immune from the stoppage of supplies from abroad, came to nothing, an effort that cost Simms personally rather more than £31,000'.

All was not lost, however, for early in 1914 Simms visited the USA where, in 1910 in East Orange, New Jersey, the Simms Magneto Company Ltd had been established. This concern was started solely to import magnetos from Britain but, because it was considered that units for the US market needed to be made in the USA, a manufacturing plant was established in 1912 at Watsersing, New Jersey. The outbreak of war and the drying up of German Bosch supplies for Britain and France gave the company the shot in the arm it needed. The plant accordingly prospered, continuing production until it was acquired by Bendix Aviation shortly after the war.

Below: truck and trailer designs were popular in the steam wagon era as illustrated by this Leyland steamer and trailer built in 1914

Bottom left: Some idea of the conditions which trucks had to contend with at the front in Flanders can be gauged from this photograph of German infantry moving up to the line

Bottom right: a 1916 Renault GZ four-cylinder troop carrier

In 1913, before he had set out for the USA, Simms had once again set up a company to make vehicle components. This was Simms Motor Units Ltd which later was to become famous not only for its magnetos but also for its fuel injection equipment for diesels. Accordingly, when war came and Bosch magneto supplies ceased, the company not only was able to manufacture magnetos in Britain but could also import them in quantity from its American plant to satisfy the clamorous demands of the British, French and Italian vehicle manufacturers. An interesting corollary to this exercise, however, was the fact that these imports into Britain from the USA were liable to heavy customs dues, and it was only strong representations from Simms that led to them being lifted from these strategic materials.

In 1914, however, Britain was prepared for war in other ways. Two years before, the War Office in London had organised what were known as the Subsidised Vehicle Trials. These were held so as to create a suitable pool of motor vehicles in the Army Reserve for use in the event of war. There were two vehicle classes, for 1½-ton and 3-ton load carriers. Vehicles which came up to the required standard were certified and the owners received from the Government a purchase premium of £50 and an annual subsidy of £20 for three years, provided the vehicles were properly maintained to a standard deemed satisfactory by a War Department inspector. However, in the event of war, the owner was required to hand the vehicle over to the Government within 72 hours. It is a point of interest that both Germany and France had similar subsidy systems but offered far more favourable financial terms to those operators participating in the scheme.

As a result of the British trials, several manufacturers were to produce designs which consolidated them for many years to come as heavy vehicle producers. They included Leyland, Maudslay, Dennis, Karrier, Wolseley and Thornycroft, all producing vehicles to the 3-ton specifica-

Left: most of the British army lorries destined for use in World War I were three-tonners to meet War Office specifications. This vehicle manufactured by Hallford was typical of the machines built to meet these standards

Below: Karrier was a major supplier of trucks to the British armed forces in World War I. The photograph shows a line-up of 3 to 4-tonners painted in sombre War Department colours outside the Karrier Works

tion. It is significant that, although the nominal payload was 3 tons, in practical terms 6–7 ton loads were frequently carried seemingly without any adverse effects.

In the period of the war, AEC was the biggest single British supplier, (not the least of its output being the B series bus) building some 10,000 units for the armed forces, Wolseley and Dennis supplied around 7500 units and Leyland and Thornycroft each supplied rather more than 5000. The Leyland output figures during the war reveal not only the types of vehicles and numbers of each supplied to HM forces but they also show the tiny quantity allocated to civilian use.

Above: one of the famous RAF-type Leylands fitted out as a mobile workshop for aircraft maintenance. A total of 765 of this type were supplied to the RFC and RAF between 1915 and 1918

	1914	1915	1916	1917	1918	TOTAL
ASC general service	156	94	—	—	—	250
RAF heavy tender	75	980	1080	1123	764	4022
RAF workshop	—	75	239	225	226	765
RAF special types	6	64	190	107	257	624
Indian Army transport	20	10	97	—	—	127
Released for civil use	2	37	88	14	3	144
Total	259	1260	1694	1469	1250	5932

This table shows Leyland War Office output from August 1914, to November 1918, inclusive. It also indicates that Leyland supplied the Royal Air Force rather than the army, although much of their output originally went to the RAF's predecessor, the Royal Flying Corps. As a result, the vehicle became known as the Leyland RAF type and it is indicative of the vehicle's durability that Leyland's official history reports that several were still in commercial operation in Bombay, India, in the late 1960s!

The RAF type was originally fitted with a four-cylinder, 32hp engine (a 36hp engine was employed in later models) which had the once-common feature of a non-detachable cylinder head (a concept to be re-adopted in rather different form in the 1960s for the Leyland 500 series engine) but with plugs over each valve so that they could be removed for maintenance or replacement. An unusual aspect of the engine was the fitment of skew gears for the timing gear instead of chain drive. The vehicle had a pressed-steel section chassis, reflecting the general trend, while the brake system was unusual in that it included a water-cooled footbrake which operated on the drive shaft. Significantly, the Bosch magneto, which was offered originally as an alternative Simms and BTH units, ceased to appear on later models. One of many companies which lost its fleet of delivery vehicles within 24 hours of the outbreak of war was the famous London furnishing store of Waring and Gillow. Their vehicles were Leyland subsidy types which were immediately called in and made ready, so that they were in Avonmouth ready for embarkation within a further 24 hours. Waring and Gillow also had its own transport company in terms of personnel

Above: The RAF-type Leyland was one of the most popular trucks produced. Many were completely refurbished after the end of World War I and used in civilian work for many years subsequently

Left: MAN's first trucks were built in 1915. This vehicle built from Saurer designs featured a 37 horsepower engine and chain drive

who, as part of the army reserve, moved off to war with the same speed.

Exercises of the same kind were mounted by the leading carriers, Pickfords and Carter Paterson, whilst the AEC B series double-deck buses of the London General Omnibus Company were immediately pressed into service as troop carriers to carry their Cockney passengers, now in khaki, to the front line in Flanders. Several of them, including one called *Old Bill*, still survive as relics of those days. The need for motor vehicles in August 1914 was immediate, and several vehicle manufacturers diverted models straight off the production line to pick up troops for transport to the front.

In Britain, the subsidy system worked reasonably well but it was later criticised on the grounds that vehicles produced under it were too uniform. It was argued that they all therefore had the same design weaknesses. While this may have been true, it can equally be said that, in the war arena, uniformity had maintenance advantages; it facilitated to some degree cannibalisation of components, and offered other advantages associated with a standard design. In contrast, the French subsidy system, which did not lay down a standard but merely applied a subsidy to any suitable vehicle, generated a wide variety of military type vehicles.

American vehicles flooded into Europe as the war progressed and were welcomed for their robust qualities, especially the Macks which appealed to the British because of the particularly tough characteristics of that make. In fact, it was the British troops of World War 1 who dubbed the Mack 'the bulldog', not only because its blunt, snub-nosed appearance resembled that of a bulldog, but because it seemed to withstand the roughest treatment and overloading. It was as a result of this that, after the war, Mack introduced the Bulldog as its symbol.

One of the most notable contributions to the role of trucks in World War I was that of Fiat, for it had, just on the outbreak of the war, introduced what was to prove a famous model with the troops. The Fiat 18BL was a 3½-ton payload outfit, still with chain drive but quite advanced in other ways, for it had a windscreen (a feature which was still a rarity), drop sides and a wooden tilt frame so that a tarpaulin could cover the load. This model was produced in great quantities for the time, and output totalled 20,000 in the years from 1914 to 1921.

Top: when war broke out in 1914, civilian vehicles were immediately mobilised. The vans of Waring and Gillow, the London store, were some of the first to go. The photograph shows one of the vehicles in France with a group of 'Old Contemptibles'

Above: the Fiat 18BL army lorry, built throughout World War I, was subsequently produced until 1921

The war led directly to the foundation of some companies which are now household names in the truck making business. Two of the biggest manufacturers in the German industry built their first trucks to meet the needs of their armed forces; these were MAN (Maschinenfabrik Augsburg-Nürnberg) and Magirus. MAN's first truck was a bonneted 4/5-tonner built under licence from the Swiss Saurer concern in 1915, and using what MAN today still calls the Otto engine, a four-cylinder unit producing 37hp. Magirus started truck manufacturing in the following year, producing a powerful 3-tonner fitted with a four-cylinder 40hp engine.

Below: Mack's reputation as a tough truck was gained in World War I and stood the company in good stead on the civilian market, especially in construction work. The photograph shows a group of tippers operated by the Borough Asphalte Co of Brooklyn, New York; note the chain-driven tipping gear

Bottom: Fiat cars and trucks built for the British Army, photographed in 1915

In France in 1914, the war led directly to the establishment of Somua (Société d'Outillage Mécanique et d'Usinage d'Artillerie) with the obvious aim of building army vehicles; this was done with the backing of armament manufacturers, Schneider. In 1955, it was to become one of the most important of the French specialist heavy vehicle producers as a major component of the industrial vehicle division of Saviem, the heavy vehicle part of the Renault Group.

It could be said, too, that the Austrian firm of Steyr owes its origins to World War I for although, as munition producers, it did not manufacture a single truck in that period, the subsequent ban on munitions production imposed by the Peace Treaty caused the management to enter truck manufacture in 1920. In Italy, Lancia, in truck terms at least, was also a name which was born out of preparations for the war – its first production load carrier being an army lorry, the IZ, built in 1912.

The war saw some strange vehicles entering service. Austro-Daimler which had produced four-wheel-drive trucks from just after the turn of the century, had later entered the world of road train operation, mainly for Austrian army use, building vehicles with engines producing over 100hp to haul howitzers. Some were used with detachable road wheels so that when rail wheels were substituted, they could move as railway trains; they were to be first examples of road-rail operation. Later, this company produced a road train to a design by Porsche. This train was hauled by a massive petrol-powered vehicle, which towed a mobile generator, which in turn provided power for the hub-mounted electric motors fitted to each of the axles of trailers hauled.

Development of road trains was not confined to this one concern. In the 1900s, an Englishman named Durtnall had designed several outfits on much the same lines for military use while, in 1911, the British Daimler concern supplied a road train, which had shaft drive to a centre axle of each trailer, for use in India. All six wheels of each trailer were iron shod, with the drive wheels being not only wider than the others but fitted with strakes for better road adhesion. This was

Road trains were popular for certain types of duty in the period leading up to World War I. The photograph above shows the British Daimler road train supplied in 1911 for military use in India. It employed a novel system of shaft drive to the wheels of each trailer. The illustration below shows a traction engine hauling several trailers in a way closely associated with rail movement

based on the French Renard system which, like the Daimler, involved the use of a powerful tractor unit to haul the trailers, each of which had a powered axle; the power to each axle was transmitted by a longitudinal flexible shaft and flexible couplings. Again, the steering was operated from the tractor unit.

One of the immediate effects of the war was the direction by European governments of factories to war production. This was of great significance not only for the British and French but also for the American truck industry. Vehicle and motor components firms in Britain, for example, switched production to such fields as armoured car, aircraft, gun and

Below: two twin-rear-wheeled Karriers undergoing trials before war service

Far right: famous car builders, Napier, built many small trucks for war work

munition production. A case in point was the English Guy Motors concern which had only started production in 1914 but was forced to switch to aero engines, successfully producing the Wasp and Dragonfly radial engines. Similarly, whilst Karrier were producing 2000 4-tonners for the war effort, they also produced large numbers of tank components.

There was, however, a seemingly insatiable demand for vehicles and this could only be met from one source so far as the Allies were concerned, the USA. The role of Mack has already been mentioned, but that of other leading manufacturers was equally productive. GMC supplied some 8500 vehicles for military use, mainly the Model 23 1-ton truck. To achieve this output, 90% of the organisation's total resources were geared to military vehicle production, an achievement which merited a War Department citation. A version of the Model 23 was also supplied in quantity to the Army Air Force, and the company's 16AA military ambulance became standard equipment with the US Army. A total of 16,000 of the Model 23 was built, making it a very successful model in terms of production by the standards of the time.

Some American truck manufacturers had already had a foretaste of providing machinery for war use, through the Mexican border campaign against Pancho Villa in 1915 and 1916. Dodge recalls that, in addition

to the Dodge staff car of General Pershing which was involved in this campaign, there were some 250 of his trucks used as troop carriers and being operated over terrain considered murderous even for today's vehicles. Predictably after this experience, many Dodge vehicles found their way to the Allied Expeditionary Force in France, the versions delivered including troop carriers, combat machines, screen-sided panel trucks and ambulances.

International Harvester was naturally also a major supplier of vehicles to the American forces. One of its main models was its series F 1-tonner, the bonneted front end of which strongly resembled the French Renault design, as indeed did most International Harvesters of this period. International Harvester in fact built over 9000 vehicles in the boom year of 1918, when the US industry as a whole produced well over 200,000 machines. White in 1918 built over 10,000 vehicles and in fact built around double that number for the US Forces in the war period. Despite these impressive numbers, in the same year, the US market leader was the Quad, made by the Nash Corporation, and whose production exceeded 11,000 vehicles. The early success of this Wisconsin-based company was remarkable, the first vehicles having come off the line shortly before the outbreak of the war in Europe. Strangely, the production levels of this company, which was later to become part of the American Motors Corporation, declined in subsequent years as quickly as they had built up, the company ceasing to produce trucks altogether in the late 1920s, although they did stage a revival in World War II. The Quad models ranged up to 2 tons load capacity and a feature of them was four-wheel drive. Their success in wartime points to the fact that one of the notable results of World War I was the quick appreciation of the benefits of four-wheel drive in rough muddy conditions. Another company which benefitted considerably from this was, of course, FWD – also of Wisconsin – which sold large numbers of a 3-tonner with four-wheel drive to the US Army. It had a three-speed gearbox and a two-speed transfer box and the robust nature of the vehicle in which they were fitted established a norm for the company which was to continue into World War II and beyond.

Wisconsin can perhaps be regarded as the home of the four-wheel-drive vehicle for it was here too that the Oshkosh (from the town of the same name) appeared, about the time when the US entered World War I as an all-wheel-drive truck maker.

Obviously, during the war, governments experimented widely and some research work which was then undertaken (like that of Ricardo on engines for tanks, for example) had a long-term beneficial impact for the truck manufacturing industry. Other investigations, however, gave no long-term benefits. Producer gas was, of course, used extensively as a vehicle fuel in civilian application but was quickly abandoned when petrol supplies started to flow again.

Rubber tyre shortage, coupled with the need for better traction, prompted attempts to design a wheel which made use of numerous metal plates backed by springs to form the 'tread'. Like Boydell's efforts with traction engines some fifty years before, these innovations were doomed to failure. One of the most significant forward thrusts to be made in the war was in this field (although not in connection with trucks) through the widespread adoption of tracks for tanks and other vehicles.

In the period when all eyes were on the war in Europe, there were, of course, changes taking place in vehicle design. On lighter vehicles, the transition from chain to shaft drive accelerated; glass windscreens made their debut and fitment of electric lighting equipment on vehicles, pioneered in the immediate pre-war years by the British Lucas concern, started to replace acetylene units which were, however, to remain the norm well into the 1920s. The benefits of pneumatic tyres were also

Far right: A converted London bus, used as a pigeon transporter for carrier pigeons, operating in camouflage paint as a travelling loft at Pernes on the Western Front in June 1918

Near right, above: An early GMC articulated vehicle. The relatively long wheelbase of the tractor unit and short deck length of the semi-trailer were common characteristics of many early artics

Near right, below: German transport columns on the march in the spring of 1918 offensive in Picardy

Below: American and French ammunition trains being rushed to the Western Front in July 1918

being increasingly realised for lighter load carriers, although solid tyres were to remain on heavies for some time yet.

Not every country involved in World War I had from the outset taken the truck as a serious weapon, but all were doing so by the end of the war. It seems strange now, but the USA did not seem fully to appreciate the motor vehicle's strategic importance until the Europeans had been involved for some time in the struggle. The US Army did not hold its first vehicle trials until 1912 and then they were only relatively minor affairs and a proper policy does not appear to have been established until around 1916, when the United States was about to enter the conflict.

By the time the Peace Treaty was signed, the major powers not only had government departments with experts concerned solely with the purchase of military vehicles and equipment but some had moved a a step further, establishing a function geared to the development of vehicles for military use.

This recognised the fact that the war had led people to realise that military needs were quite different from those governing the design and use of trucks for commerce. The war had shown that the military need was largely for vehicles with robust chassis, offering a high ground clearance, versatility, strong suspension and a rough terrain capability. In contrast, the commercial need was for high payload (something which did not matter so much with military vehicles), economy of operation (which mattered virtually not at all in military use) and the ability to travel at optimum speeds under the varying traffic conditions encountered on the public highway.

When peace came it was to be legal requirements, road improvements and design improvements to match these circumstances which were to mould the truck manufacturing and operating industries.

Below left: a hotch-potch of vehicles was used in World War I for supplying the troops in France. This photograph shows a Leyland steam wagon and an AEC B type bus converted to a lorry being loaded with meat

Right: this photograph of an early cab interior reveals the primitive conditions afforded to drivers. This one had a wind windscreen but otherwise there is an obvious lack of creature comforts

Far right: built in 1918, this White truck was operated by the Tacoma Railway and Power Co Ltd, of Tacoma, Washington

Below: a 1917 Pierce army truck; note the ample ground clearance

64

CHAPTER 3

The Industry Expands

The after-affects of World War I on the world's motor industry were immediate and far reaching. The German truck manufacturing industry, although faced with an acute petrol shortage, could have been much harder hit than it was in reality. Because commercial vehicles were not classed as war material, they were not part of the disarmament plan imposed on Germany. In fact, several of the big armament companies which were no longer allowed to produce war material, but had plenty of spare production facilities, turned their eyes to truck manufacture. The most notable name in this respect was Krupp which built its first truck in 1920, a chain-driven 5-tonner.

France was left with a ravaged countryside along its northern frontier and for miles behind it, and thousands of army trucks now surplus to requirements. These included not only French vehicles but captured German ones and many American vehicles which were not proposed to be shipped back to the USA. Quite a few of these were, however, disposed of in Britain with the result that there are today still quite a number left in the hands of collectors. Many of these war-surplus vehicles were sold off to returning veterans who set up on their own account as transport contractors. Contemporary British statistics reveal the extent of this haulage boom. In 1918, there were less than 400 licensed road haulage undertakings; by 1923, there were over 2400. By then, too, there were 180,000 trucks on British roads, more than double the figure for 1918.

The potential of road transport had been revealed to many by the war and the market was ripe to accept it as the railways were suffering not only from the strain imposed on them by their war efforts but an obsolete system of rail freight charges. Road transport with low overheads started undercutting rail tariffs and a new war had started which was to be fought fiercely for the next fifty years, not only in Britain but in every country in the world.

In the immediate post-war period, truck manufacturers were obviously worried about the impact of the sale of ex-War Department vehicles, which had obviously been well used. Leyland took the step of buying all Leyland war stock that it could trace and reconditioning them before re-sale at a factory bought for this purpose at Kingston on Thames. Over 3000 vehicles were bought and reconditioned in this way; it nearly ruined the firm financially, but may have saved them from a nasty reputation.

Most vehicles, however, went as they were into the hands of dealers. It is an interesting point that, as some dealers in Britain specialised in particular makes, it followed that ex-wartime American vehicles constituted the main product line. This happened with Peerless, for

Left: the Model T Ford of 1919 had a load capacity of 1-ton and was powered by a 3-litre petrol engine; like the Model T car, it was cheap and reliable

example, and when the stock ran out, amounting to thousands of vehicles and parts, the firm started to manufacture the make in Britain, such was the strength of the name.

In Britain in the early 1920s, however, steam wagons were still significant in heavy work, and it was only when the flood of ex-War Department petrol-engined vehicles poured on to the market did the steamer's decline start, hastened by oppressive legislation, with the final death blow being administered by the successful adaptation of the diesel to automotive use. Even Foden, one of the most successful of the steam wagon producers, decided in 1929 to build diesel vehicles and abandon its steamers. By then, of course, most of the other steam wagon producers had gone bankrupt, closed down, or diversified into other activities. One of the last arrivals on the steamer scene, Atkinson, which produced its first steam wagon in 1916 and enjoyed expanding market conditions for the next seven years, ran into financial problems in the late 1920s and the company crashed. It is ironic that before this happened, Edward Atkinson, the founder and managing director, was offered £75,000 in cash for the business and the position of Managing Director for life. He turned it down indicating that if the business was worth that much to those people making the offer it was worth more to him. Things got worse, however, and he lost complete control when the company was placed in the hands of the Official Receiver in 1930. The company soldiered on under this control largely as a service company until a London businessman, W.G. Allen, bought it and formed Atkinson Lorries (1933) Ltd. From that point on, Atkinsons never looked back, building high quality diesel vehicles until amalgamation with Seddon Diesel Vehicles in 1971 and acquisition of Seddon-Atkinson by International Harvester in 1975.

Steamer payloads at the beginning of the 1920s were 6 to 7 tons and exceptionally 10 to 12 tons – still substantially more than petrol-engined machines, where a 7 to 8 ton payload was still a rarity. Bigger vehicles were on the way, and the first six-wheeled rigid designs started to appear on the European scene from companies like Thornycroft in Britain and MAN and Mercedes-Benz in Germany. Offering a normal payload of 10 to 12 tons, they were yet another nail in the coffin of steam wagons. In the meantime, an even bigger nail had been hammered in by the first real articulated vehicles, also of course six-wheelers. They were usually called 'flexibles', to distinguish them from 'rigids'.

Scammell, now part of the Leyland Group, is an important name in commercial vehicle history because it is fair to say that this company was responsible for much of the pioneer work on the concept and development of the articulated vehicle. Scammell Lorries Ltd was founded in 1921 at the time of the post-war slump but, in the days before World War I, G. Scammell and Nephew Ltd, based at Fashion Street, Spitalfields in London, built up a substantial business selling and maintaining steam wagons and small trucks. When the war came, it was recognised that mechanical transport had a vast potential, and the practical experience gained of pulling trailers in the war was subsequently put to use. The result was the first Scammell artic in 1919. On test in the following year, it pulled a load of just under 8 tons up West Hill, Highgate, London and reached 18mph on the flat.

In the 1920s, Scammell developed a formidable reputation not only in Britain but worldwide for its heavy haulage designs. As a point of interest, they were one of the last concerns to abandon chain drive, producing heavy vehicles with this means of transmission well into the 1930s. Contrary to popular belief, chain drive was used on some ultra-heavy vehicles, particularly in the USA, right up to the years following World War II. Scammell's arrival on the articulated vehicle scene marked the beginning of a wave of interest in this type of vehicle, and

Below: a 1919 Oldsmobile 30hp 1-tonner which was fitted with such luxuries as a glass windscreen, electric lighting and pneumatic tyres; its engine is detailed on the right

others emulated Scammell. In England, AEC launched its first artic – a 10-tonner based upon the company's 4-ton truck design – and in France they appeared from Chenard and Walcker and Latil. The German industry did not take much interest in articulated vehicles, obviously preferring even at this early stage the lorry-and-drawbar-trailer concept which was to characterise German long-distance haulage for the next three decades. It is perhaps significant that, even at that time, the Germans were using air brakes on these road trains which seem to have owed a great deal in this design to railway train braking principles.

In America at that time, while most of the leading truck producing companies like Mack and GMC were still concentrating on four-wheeler production, a handful, like International Harvester, built their first articulate units. Rigid 6 × 2 and 6 × 4 chassis started to make their appearance there, too. The US Army had a notable pro-

Below: this White model 40 3½-ton truck built in 1921 was the first model for civilian use built by White after the success of its designs in World War I

gramme of converting some of the ex-World War I Liberty trucks first to 6 × 2 outfits and then 6 × 4, which was to have a long-term impact on design concepts. After the war, the Goodyear Company developed a double drive bogie with braking on all four wheels, and a major contribution to the 6 × 4 rigid concept was made by the Hendrickson concern in 1924 when it developed the Hendrickson bogie, featuring two axles coupled by a centrally pivoting underslung beam, which was to become world famous in the years to come.

In the mid 1920s, the move to six-wheeled rigid designs was encouraged by pneumatic tyre development. There was a constant demand for higher payloads, and ten tons on a four-wheeler meant tyre blowouts. But fitment of pneumatics was being encouraged by governments who had found that when they were fitted there was far less damage to the road surface; so, to spread the load, a third axle was desirable. Overloaded pneumatics had a nasty habit of exploding on vehicles run at speed over long distances. Another of the problems with early six-wheeled rigids was tyre scrub which manufacturers tried to minimise on these early units by fitting single-tyred wheels sometimes ahead, and sometimes behind, doubles.

Apart from the Hendrickson development, there was a widely different approach adopted to six-wheeler design. In 1924, Büssing produced a six-wheeler with separate drives to the two rear axles from a step-down gearbox after the main gearbox. The British Caledon concern built a six-wheeler with a live axle driving two dead ones by chains. In the same year, Karrier produced designs with two underworm back axles, and in 1927 Associated Daimler made what was termed the London Six, a six-wheeled bus chassis with a double reduction worm bogie; another intriguing double reduction design came from the

Swiss firm of Brozincevic & Co of Zurich, on a 10-tonner. Leyland's Terrier six-wheeler design of 1927 was so well thought of that it was accepted for the British War Department's subsidy scheme – with essentially similar models from rival makers.

By this time, worldwide, manufacturers were committed to bonneted designs, although there were notable exceptions like Renault who in 1923 launched a 20hp forward control 4-tonner.

There was a renewed flurry of interest in the immediate post-war years in the petrol-electric vehicle. In Britain, the main manufacturer in this field was Tilling-Stevens of Maidstone (absorbed later into the Rootes Group and then Chrysler), whose model of the early 1920s was fitted with an engine driving a 25kw dynamo which in turn powered an electric motor to drive the rear wheels. There were many people who felt this principle had a big future, for it offered quiet running and a much smoother drive through the absence of clutch and gearbox and thus transmission shock. Driving was easier, braking better and there was the bonus of electric power being available for ancillary operations. However, it lacked the lively performance which characterised the petrol engined vehicle and had virtually faded from the picture by the end of the decade despite the fact that, later, other manufacturers tried

Below right: petrol-electrics had their supporters in the early days of the motor truck. This is one of the famous designs, the Tilling-Stevens, built at Maidstone, Kent, in the early 1920s

Below left: the move to six-wheeled rigid trucks in the 1920s was widespread. This is a Leyland Terrier 1-ton 6 x 4 built by Leyland for heavy duty applications

Bottom: there were many experiments with electric delivery vehicles from the 1900s into the 1920s and have been periodically since. Harrods, the famous London Department store, operated a large fleet of electrics of this type for many years

their hand at this type of vehicle. In Germany in 1927 for example, Büssing produced a petrol-electric six-wheeler with separate motors and prop shafts.

The post-war truck manufacturing boom, experienced particularly in Britain, was short-lived. By 1920, as the ex-forces vehicles hit the market and a world economic depression set in, many truck manufacturing companies ran into financial difficulties. One of the early victims in England was Commer who had a receiver put in to handle the company's affairs in 1922 but managed to struggle on until taken over by Humber Ltd in 1925, thus to become part of the Rootes Group. When that organisation took over a few years later, Commer was one of the lucky ones, and a number of others, particularly in Britain and the USA, were out of business by the end of the 1920s. Some, like Karrier, attempted to ward off problems by moving inso specialist markets – in their case municipal vehicles. Leyland was also a company which ran into trouble. They had sold in foreign markets since long before the war, but in 1919 began a vigorous policy of overseas expansion which in the long term would make the company the world's biggest truck and bus exporter. Offices were opened in Sydney, Australia, and in Wellington, New Zealand. A Toronto, Canada, branch was established and agencies established throughout India and the East and South Africa. However, they could not have hit a worse time. Australia had one of its worst-ever droughts followed by terrible floods. In India, there was a major financial crisis which had a damaging effect on the company and which also led to the failure of Leyland's South African agents. Then, depression hit at home. Leyland missed its dividend, stock values dropped and very soon the company, reduced in size, was working a four-day fortnight. The massive adverse balance in the company accounts incurred took several years (and an almost total change of management!) to pay off before the company was on an even keel again.

Below: one of the first 10-ton load carriers, this six-wheeled Leyland of the 1920s had by this time been equipped with a windscreen; the sides of the cab were still open to the elements, however

Above: large numbers of ex-wartime American trucks were to be found on British roads in the 1920s. This is an ex US Army Liberty of 1924

Above right: hydraulically operated tippers started to make their debut in quantity in the 1920s. This smart Leyland had a 6-ton capacity and when produced was, from the note on the chassis, limited to 12mph

Other companies tried diversification and this in hindsight could have been the move that saved General Motors, which had by no means an easy time in the 1920s. GM points out that, as a company, it was for instance quick to recognise disadvantages in depending wholly upon outside sources for parts. The first exclusive parts manufacturing

unit to join General Motors (in 1910) was Jackson-Church-Wilcox, forerunner of the Saginaw Steering Gear Division, followed in the same year by the Champion Ignition Company, now the AC Spark Plug Division. The real consolidation took place as World War I ended, however, for in 1918 United Motors Corporation joined GM. This organisation included the Dayton Engineering Laboratories, Remy Electric, Klaxon, Harrison Radiator, Jaxon Steel Products, Hyatt Roller Bearing, New Departure and United Motor Service companies. Also in 1918, the GM lines of cars were augmented by Chevrolet, and in the following year Fisher Body became affiliated with GM. Nevertheless, 1920 saw GM in financial difficulties and it was not until the era of Alfred P. Sloan Jr, who assumed the GM presidency in 1923, that today's giant was put on course. He recognised GM's basic organisational problems and created a new concept of management philosophy. To achieve the balance necessary for flexible operation, he established GM management on a foundation of centralised policy and decentralised administration.

The 1920s also saw one of GMs most important acquisitions – Vauxhall Motors, manufacturers of Bedford trucks. The Bedford name goes back to the Bedford Motor Co of Willesden, North London, which in 1912 supplied bodywork for Buick chassis imported from the USA by General Motors. In 1925, GM bought Vauxhall Motors Ltd, and began to make commercial vehicles at Luton. The first ones to be built were the Chevrolet LQs, which were of 12cwt and 30cwt carrying capacity and incorporated a then new six-cylinder engine – petrol of course – which, with few changes, remained the basic engine for Chevrolet cars until 1953.

Mention of Ford raises the point that up to the end of World War I the company had concentrated primarily on car production. It had, of course, produced light goods carrying vehicles for some time but as derivatives of the famous model T car chassis and its forebears. The usual maximum load capacity at this stage was 1 ton (although there were $\frac{1}{2}$ ton, $\frac{3}{4}$ ton and $1\frac{1}{2}$-ton versions), which of course made it suitable for a wide variety of delivery duties. Wood spoked wheels and rims were the norm and, strangely perhaps, pneumatic tyres were employed on the front wheels and solids on the back in goods applications. The only other major concession to goods carrying appears to have been heavy duty rear springs. This period, too, was one of expansion of the US truck making industry into purpose-built factories with advanced production lines. Typical in this respect was International Harevster who in 1923 had its first vehicle come off the line at a brand new plant at Fort Wayne, Indiana. International Harvester claims to have had the biggest volume truck production in the USA at that time, and that means the biggest in the world.

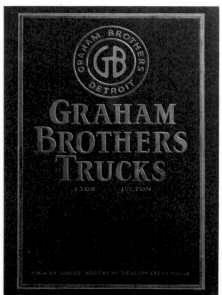

Above : a truck dealer's sign of 1924 advertising a name which, today, is one more for the history books, although the name of Dodge with which the company became associated in this year lives on

One of the modern giants changed hands several times in the 1920s. This was Dodge whose screen-sided panel trucks developed in the war were popular after the war in civilian use. In 1920, both the founders of the business, John and Horace Dodge, died. At this time, commercial vehicle chassis accounted for 10% of Dodge's total volume, but by 1925 this figure had doubled largely through an association with the Graham Brothers of Evansville, Indiana, who built truck bodies on the Dodge commercial chassis. In this year, Graham Brothers joined with Dodge and vehicles produced became known as Graham Brothers Trucks. Later that same year, the company was bought by Dillon, Read & Company, a New York Banking firm by whom it was run until 1928 when Chrysler Corporation bought the company. In spite of the depression years that followed, the Dodge operation continued to be successful.

Of the European truck industry operating in 1914, one sector was to

Left: the Dodge name could have disappeared without a trace in 1924 when a merger resulted in the Graham Bros name being used. The photograph shows a 1924 Series B Graham 1-tonner being unloaded at a grain store

Below: a Ford TT Dumper of 1925. This 20hp vehicle, with its Jumbo Giant transmission, had a top speed of 35mph

Bottom: another TT Ford, this time in 1923 Railroad-goods-carrying guise

be so hard hit that it never really recovered after the war: the old Austro-Hungarian empire. The manufacturers included Skoda, Praga and Tatra in the then new Czechoslovakia, Raba in Hungary and the many producers of Austria itself like Austro Daimler, Graf & Stift, the Austrian Saurer company and Steyer. Some, like Austro Daimler, disappeared completely as truck producers. OAF, originally producing Fiat trucks, also ceased making lorries but started again in the 1930s, this time associated with MAN. The other Austrian producers soldiered on very much in the way of Skoda, Praga and Tatra, but not as the force they had once been. The French truck industry in contrast continued as a worldwide force although perhaps there were not the notable achievements that had characterised the French industry of the early 1900s. Berliet consolidated on the success of its wartime models with an expanded new range of vehicles as did De Dion Bouton and Renault. Peugeot flirted with heavy truck production but ended up with a line of light vehicle models, while Unic moved from car to truck manufacture. New names appeared on the French truck-making scene. These included Citroën, which was to become a force in the light vehicle market with its car derivatives first produced in 1920. Laffly (now part of the Saviem group) and Willeme, were founded, both moving directly into 3-ton – 5-ton truck manufacture, Laffly around 1922 and Willeme immediately after the war. Finally, there came Bennes Basculantes Bernard, which was formed as a tipper vehicle producer, later to become Camions Bernard. The Bernard name was to continue right up to the late 1950s when its plant was acquired by Mack Trucks for part of its European assembly operations.

A leader in the truck world of today got off to a late start in 1927: Volvo, of Gothenburg, Sweden. The first Volvo truck was a modest 1½-

Below: it was in the 1920s that Morris decided to diversify from its highly successful range of motor cars into light-truck production, its first model being a 1-tonner. This one, built in 1926, was designed for refuse collection

Bottom: a 1924 Mack Bulldog 6-tonner which was powered by a 68bhp engine

tonner fitted with a 40hp petrol engine and a crash gearbox. Volvo recalls that the necessary double declutching system made it difficult to handle, particularly in the case of new and inexperienced drivers. This first model, the LV40, was followed in 1929 by the company's first six-cylinder engined truck, which was matched with a four-speed gearbox.

As some companies switched from truck to car production in the 1920s, so some car producers diversified into truck manufacture. One of the most significant moves in these terms was that made in Britain in 1924 by Morris Cars Ltd with the formation of Morris Commercial Cars Ltd. The vehicle it produced was a 1-tonner with the Morris four-cylinder petrol engine as fitted in the largest model in the Morris car range. Three years later, two lightweight double drive six-wheelers were added with payloads of 1½ and 2 tons, the company building a strong basis in light truck design which was to continue through to the period of the 1950s when the company joined up with the Austin Motor Co (primarily a car producer in the 1920s, although it had made a strange commercial chassis with twin propeller shafts before the War) as the British Motor Corporation.

There was a growing truck making industry by countries new to vehicle manufacture, notably Japan. Japan had, of course, fought alongside Britain and the USA in World War I and Japanese truck production dates from the end of hostilities in 1918. Hino Motors and Isuzu Motors of Tokyo, both started truck production in that year, Hino producing what it terms Japan's first original motor vehicle in that year, the Model TGE A-type truck. Both companies expanded in the 1920s, with Isuzu starting to make vehicles of its own design under the name Sumida in 1928 and Hino in the same year marketing its new ranges of E and L-type trucks.

Mitsubishi Motors Corporation moved into car production in 1917, concentrating on light truck production in the 1920s. In this decade, too, the Soviet Union started seriously to consider truck manufacture.

Before World War I, the Russian truck industry was virtually non-existent. However, in the 1920s, the first moves came with the launch of a small truck from a Moscow plant. A bonneted 1½-tonner, it had a four-cylinder 35bhp engine. Larger vehicles of similar design followed of 2½, 4 and 5 tons carrying capacity in the period from 1926 on.

Economic forces started to operate early in the 1930s which were to influence the worldwide pattern of development of the truck industry for many years to come, and they were not just those associated with the Wall Street crash of 1929 and the world slump. Most of the leading truck-producing countries had introduced, or were introducing, legislation at this time to check the erosion of rail goods traffic. Licensing systems for truck operations and other checks to truck use, including fiscal ones, were imposed. Measures to protect railway systems were extreme, and today, for example, still underlie transport policy in countries like France and Germany. It was also an era in which the future importance of good road systems was realised. Here, the USA was well in the lead with its interstate highway system, the US Government's enlightened attitude to the 'good roads' movement of the 1920s paying off for road transport companies. The first moves to purpose-built road networks were seen in Europe, too, with Germany building the first European motor roads.

Right up to today, the road-rail conflict and motor road development between main industrial centres and ports have exerted strong influences on truck design. Only in more recent years have equally important influences developed, like those associated with international freight container use, the oil crisis and environmental issues.

There had been a fantastic growth in the truck population in the 1920s. In Britain alone between 1919 and 1929, goods vehicles operating

Below: contrasting styles in truck advertising are revealed here; Stewart Motor Trucks was obviously selling its product by lots of detail, while Renault concentrated on its famous name

commercially rose from 62,000 to 330,000. In the 1930s, the rate of expansion in Britain slowed with the total reaching 488,000 in 1939, but these numbers were chicken feed compared with America. The American truck industry dwarfed that of the world: by 1939, there were eight times as many trucks on US roads as in Britain and the UK then had the second biggest truck park in the world; Germany had around 250,000 goods vehicles, France just over 400,000, while Japan's truck park was around 50,000! The USA was by a long way the biggest truck exporter, too, although Britain had markets in Australia, New Zealand, South Africa, India and the Far East, and many other territories in the Middle East and Africa. France and, to a lesser extent, Italy had similar overseas markets in their colonies; German exports were mainly to other European countries.

World depression marked the opening of the 1930s and, as in the early 1920s, many truck operators went out of business. Everyone was looking for maximum economy in running vehicles and, in Europe especially, the right climate was created for the acceptance of diesels. Fuel economy was sought above all else, with this factor outweighing the many disadvantages of the early diesel engines. Most of these engines were massive units compared with the modern automotive diesel, and they were noisy smelly, and the vibration they generated for the driver would nowadays be considered unacceptable.

The interest in diesels was not confined to Germany, Britain and the USA. Fiat in Italy was working on automotive diesel development and had, in fact, started building diesel engines for stationary and marine application in 1908; the first Italian diesel trucks left the Fiat plants in 1931. They were the 4-ton capacity 632 N and the 6-ton 634 N, fitted with four and six-cylinder direct injection diesel engines, re-

Below: the availability of a six-cylinder engine in place of a four-cylinder unit was highlighted in this advertisement for the Chevrolet 30cwt of 1930

Bottom: divided windscreen, wing mirrors and windscreen wipers are a few of the advances to be noted in this 1933 Fiat truck and trailer outfit

76

spectively. Fiat points out that the 634, which remained in production until 1939, can be considered the most interesting diesel truck of the period. An 8310cc vehicle, developing 75bhp at 1700rpm, it had a maximum speed of 37 kph (23·125mph). This was the first Fiat vehicle with a sleeper cab, the range over which road transport now operated having extended greatly. Then, just before World War II, the company brought out two new models, the 626N (Medium) and the 666N (heavy), both forward control models with the cab positioned well ahead and above of the front axle.

France's first diesel was one produced by a firm called Martin in 1928, and the first chassis manufacturer to install a diesel appears to have been Berliet whose first vehicle appeared in 1930, once again making use of the Acro system of combustion. It was not a success and so Berliet switched to the Ricardo system which had proved so successful on British diesels, reflecting a general trend by others involved in automotive diesel construction. Renault launched its first diesel model in 1931 when it announced a bonneted $7\frac{1}{2}$ tonner, the UDD 6, the six indicating the fact that the diesel had that number of cylinders; a five-speed gearbox was fitted on this for the first time.

Some measure of the inroads of the diesel on the truck scene in the 1930s is revealed in the book *Marius Berliet L'Inflexible,* by Saint Loup, which indicates that, in the first eleven months of 1939, Berliet's Venissieux plant produced no less than 7870 automotive diesel engines.

As the decade moved towards its close, the numbers of European manufacturers producing or fitting diesels became legion – Thornycroft, Panhard, Somua, Unic, Büssing Henschel, Krupp, Magirus Deutz, Alfa Romeo, OM, Scania and Volvo. Some of the engines were produced under licence usually from the Swiss Saurer company or the German Lanova and Junkers companies or the British Gardner and Perkins concerns. As a point of interest, some of the first Japanese diesels were built on the Junkers two-stroke diesel patent by Nihon Diesel Industries (later Nissan Diesel Motor Co Ltd) of Tokyo in 1935.

Scania turned over completely to diesel trucks in 1935 and joined the select group of all-diesel truck producers – following the move made by MAN three years earlier which had been swiftly followed by companies like ERF, Seddon, Atkinson and Foden in Britain.

Of the European companies mentioned earlier, Magirus Deutz was perhaps the most unusual, for they were working on air-cooled diesels which in fact they did not start fitting in quantity in vehicles until 1940. It was to be an effective move and no other company has been able to produce anything like as successful an air-cooled automotive diesel power unit, although many have tried.

One of those which was successful was the Japanese Isuzu concern which launched a 5·3-litre air-cooled diesel in 1936 which fitted in its heaviest range of trucks. It was in this year, too, that the Mitsubishi Motors Corporation launched its first diesel truck – a year after building its first diesel bus; these were not air-cooled designs, however.

In the USA, at this stage, Cummins was the principle developer of the diesel, although GM was also working hard on developing its two-stroke design. In 1932, the Model H Cummins was introduced, and was rated at 85bhp. It was fitted in a truck carrying a 17,750lb payload and ran round the Indianapolis speedway to establish a record by clocking 14,600 miles non-stop at an average speed of 43·397mph. Not long after this, the same engine, installed in a Mack bus, was used in a speed run over 3200 miles. However, Cummins did not make a profit until 1937 when the merits of long engine life and inexpensive operation were realised. Meanwhile, GM's two-stroke was installed in a rail wagon for the first time in 1934, and the Detroit Diesel Engine Division was organised to produce industrial and automotive diesels in 1937.

Cummins engines found favour in the 1930s with a number of companies, including International Harvester, Diamond T, Mack, FWD, Oshkosh, Kenworth and White. Mack, incidentally, also fitted Mercedes-Benz engines experimentally, and Zenon Hansen in his *Legend of the Bulldog* refers to the exhaustive testing carried out on diesels by Mack in the 1930s which resulted eventually in the company producing its own compression-ignition engine in 1938.

However, the 1930s in the USA were marked less by diesel fitment than the development of increasingly powerful straight-six petrol engines. The seemingly limitless supply of cheap petrol in America at this time limited diesel use quite markedly right up to the late 1960s. In fact, when US engine manufacturers looked at the diesel-for-petrol-replacement market in Europe in the 1960s, they found there was not one, although diesel re-power was booming in the USA. The first successful Vee petrol engines appeared in light trucks in the 1930s, the most notable, perhaps, being the Ford V8, a four-cylinder 24hp unit developing 50bhp at 2600rpm.

In the 1930s, too, it was obvious that some lessons of World War I had not been lost on Germany, notably German dependence on imported fuel. Adolf Hitler pushed diesel development hard with the result that in 1939, the German truck industry, and most of its fighting vehicles for that matter, were diesel powered. Petrol-powered vehicles were at a minimum and, with the Fischer Tropsch process of converting soft coal into liquid hydrocarbons having given the German industry a source of petrol (albeit limited), German fuel imports were at the minimum level possible when war came in September 1939.

There were other developments in the 1930s apart from those centred on power units. The rigid six-wheeler boom which started in the 1920s

Below: a four-cylinder 40hp Autocar truck which made an excellent light vehicle for farm work

Below right: an unusual mixture – a Willys Overland Crossley of 1928

Bottom centre: the Bedford name started to creep into the picture in 1931 in this Chevrolet advertisement. Soon, Bedford was to start producing and advertising in its own right

Bottom right: 1931 was the year when the Foden steam age ended; this is their last ever steamer

continued into this period, and it was inevitable perhaps that fourth axles on vehicles should be considered. By this time, most countries had legislation laying down maximum axle, gross and unladen weight limits while in some countries, notably Britain, the legal requirements encouraged the use of multi-axled rigid (as opposed to articulated) machines. Companies like Foden, Atkinson, AEC, Maudslay, Scammell, Thornycroft and Leyland all started offering eight-wheelers.

It was in 1934 that Leyland was to produce perhaps the most famous eight-wheeler of all, the Octopus, a 14½ ton payload machine which, improved steadily over the years, was not to disappear until the UK laws were changed in 1964. Its main rival was the AEC Mammoth Major, a vehicle offering a similar payload. The Octopus had twin steering axles and, from it, were developed two twin-steer three axle

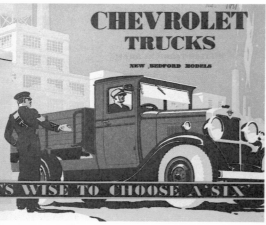

designs called the Steer and the Gnu, neither of which could be considered successful.

Use of articulated vehicles increased steadily but not spectacularly in the 1930s, but especially in the USA where the emphasis was on tractor units with surprisingly long wheelbases by today's standards. This was due to the fact that an extremely long bonnet had to be accommodated. To the modern eye, with what is now known about weight distribution and steering characteristics, artics of this period look unstable – they were, but then so were many drawbar trailer outfits. Nevertheless, with the growth of inter-state hauling in the USA, rigid vehicles hauling two or three trailers increased, and the decade marked the use of the first double bottoms – articulated vehicles hauling drawbar trailers.

Braking on some of the heavier outfits at this time remained lethal by modern standards. Use of the drawbar trailer was popular but a second

PLEASE DON'T
LITTER THE STREETS

man was required by law in some countries mainly to apply the trailer brakes. This was an unsatisfactory situation which continued for a long time in some places. Drivers of that period recall that when descending steep gradients it was not uncommon to see a vehicle overtaking on

the off-side only to realise that it was the outfit's own trailer sliding by. It was to take the industry another thirty years to minimise the problem of trailer swing and thus reduce the incidence of jack-knifing of articulated vehicles.

Several peculiar three-wheeled tractor units for articulated vehicle use made their debut in the early 1930s. Scammell introduced the Mechanical Horse, a three-wheeled tractor unit with one front wheel and two rear designed for urban duties, which was later to be called the Scarab. It became popular all over the world, particularly with railways for rail terminal collection and delivery, and thousands were made, the design steadily improving with the years until it was phased out early in the 1970s. At around the same time, Karrier developed a similar machine called the Cob for the same kind of work but this lasted a much shorter time than the Scammell design. Karrier, incidentally, was acquired in 1934 by Rootes Securities which moved the company's production to a joint operation with Commer at Luton.

An even more unusual three-wheeled tractor design was the Tug, a variant of the Ford Model Y range introduced in 1935. This had the same driver's cab as that on the 5cwt vans and private cars but a single wheel replaced the front axle and the rear axle moved forward to a position just behind the driver's seat, the cab being chopped off from the normal body at that point to accommodate an automatic coupling gear over the axle. Ford had a happy knack in those days of providing small articulated tractor units by shortening wheelbases of existing truck designs and mounting coupling gear on what was left of the chassis to haul sometimes quite long semi-trailers! This tendency to convert rather than purpose-build seems to have been normal with Fords at that time. On a bonneted six-wheeler, which was grandly called the Square Deal Stake Body Twin-flex Six Wheel Brake Four Wheel Drive Truck (which says it all), the four-wheel driven characteristic of the bogie fitted was achieved by chain drive from a live to a dead axle, the chain being driven on sprockets fitted to the outer hubs of each axle.

The fad for three-wheelers was not confined to tractor units for articulated work, for there was a profusion of light van design based on motor cycle principles from well known motor cycle companies like Raleigh, James, Scott and Ariel. Three-wheeled-car manufacturers, like Morgan, moved into the same market, and Reliant, who to this day produce three-wheeled vans, started manufacturing in this period. Some of the three-wheeler designs produced were very unstable – especially where the single axle was fitted below the load compartment.

It is an interesting point in these days of easy cab access on forward control urban delivery vehicles, that in the light vehicle field in the 1930s virtually all vehicles were of the bonneted type. The same was true of most medium-weight and heavy outfits, but there were exceptions, like many of the British four, six and eight-wheelers, and those of a few of the European manufacturers, like Renault in France, Hanomag in Germany and Fiat in Italy. These concerns had all found that the forward control concept enabled a much bigger load area to be accommodated. These forward control designs introduced then were to form the backbone of the European swing to forward control which took place after World War II. Of them all, the AEC and Leyland designs in Britain and the Fiat 626N in Italy were particularly notable trend-setters. In the USA, in contrast, the return to forward control was to be a post-war phenomenon, the huge numbers of bonneted US army vehicles available in the post-war period slowing down the swing to cab-over-engine designs.

It seems surprising today, but wooden-spoked wheels only finally disappeared in the early 1930s; Ford, for example, seems to have fitted them on model Ts and TTs right up until the end of the 1920s.

The 1930s saw the start of the fitment of many features of the modern truck. Sleeper cabs made their debut in both the USA and Europe; not that they were exactly comparable with their equivalents of the 1970s. A glance at the International Harvester sleeper cab of that period reveals a very spartan specification with just a transversely fitted bunk immediately behind the driver's seat. Spartan it may have been by today's standards, but it was a lot better than trying to curl up on the driver's seat as had previously been the case. One of the first sleeper cab designs in Europe came from Magirus in Germany. This was a bonneted unit, in common with the sleeper cab designs of this period, and it was introduced in 1931. Both wheelbase length and bumper-to-back-of-cab length were such that only a relatively short semi-trailer could be towed.

Power steering on heavy vehicles was also applied for the first time in this period, and Diamond T is believed to have been the first to adopt it. A handful of companies like Scammell in Britain tried rubber sus-

Below: three examples of Fiat advertising showing small, medium and heavyweight vehicles

Right: with the acceptance of the diesel engine, Foden moved successfully from steam to compression-ignition engined lorry manufacture. This four-wheeler was one of its first, built in 1933 using a Gardner engine

Bottom: in 1937, trucks were starting to get a more modern look, even though, as with these 1937 General Motor's Tippers, bonneted as opposed to forward control designs were still supreme

634 N TRASPORTO MERCI GROSSO TONNELLAGGIO AUTOCARRO CON MOTORE A NAFTA

FIAT 618 IL MODERNO VEICOLO LEGGERO PER TUTTI I SERVIZI E PER TUTTI GLI IMPIEGHI

FIAT 621 PN Portata utile 3500 Kg. L'AUTOCARRO A NAFTA ECONOM

pension on heavy vehicles for the first time, with Scammell's being fitted as the rear springing on their 8 × 2 in 1936.

Although it is easy to be critical about braking standards in the 1930s, notable advances were made in brake component design and fitment. For example, hydraulic braking was being applied to all four wheels of twin-axled medium weights by an increasing number of companies, although brakes were not always to be found on all wheels of six-wheeled rigids and multi-axled artics. In Europe, where air brakes were the norm on the bigger outfits, the arduous road conditions of mountainous regions gave rise to the first exhaust brakes to retard vehicles descending steep gradients.

Semi-automatic and automatic transmissions started being fitted to trucks, and a notable breakthrough here was by GM in 1939 with the announcement of the Hydramatic completely automatic transmission for light vehicles. There were moves in the 1930s, too, towards more sophisticated methods of truck body manufacture. Aluminium alloy was tried for the first time in the USA as a replacement for the heavy steel and hardwood panels then commonly used with hardwood framing. Chassis manufacturers, again in the USA, started to construct purpose-built truck bodies on a production line basis to offer complete vehicles as standard, instead of chassis cabs for the bodybuilder to

Previous page: Bedford established its reputation in the 1930s with reliable models like this 3-tonner of 1935

Below: articulated vehicles were starting to find increasing favour in the years immediately before World War II; this one was built by International in 1938

Below right: Fordson was the name under which Ford trucks were marketed in Britain from the 1930s into the early 1950s, as this 1936 advertisement illustrates

Bottom right: the French Latil concern built a number of rugged articulated tractors in the 1930s; this outfit was operated for many years by the sugar-refining group of Tate and Lyle

complete. In Britain the use of containers, not only for road-rail goods movement but on the short sea routes to Ireland, became commonplace, pre-empting in many ways the international freight container boom of the 1950s and 1960s.

By the 1930s, most of the truck manufacturing giants of today had finished with major upheavals, and their bases had been established – an exception was GM. Back in 1925, the General Motors Truck Company had merged with the Yellow Cab Manufacturing Company of Chicago, forming a new company called the Yellow Truck & Coach Manufacturing Company. Until 1936, the General Motors Truck Company was the sales subsidiary of Yellow Truck, while the General Motors Truck Corporation was the manufacturing subsidiary. However, in 1936, the Yellow Truck & Coach Manufacturing Company became the manufacturer of all GMC trucks, tractors, trailers, taxicabs and Yellow coaches, and sales activities were carried on by the General Motors Truck & Coach Division of the parent company.

The British latecomers to the world of truck-manufacture in the 1930s have been mentioned. There were, of course, others in various parts of the world. In the USA, one of the most important of these was

Below: on lighter trucks, the influence of car styling could be clearly seen in the 1930s, as ably shown with this 1938 vehicle from General Motors

Peterbilt who started building heavy duty outfits in 1939 in Oakland, California. The Netherlands, at much the same time, saw the first vehicle from DAF of Eindhoven. This was a peculiar 4 × 4 amphibian, built for the Dutch army, which had no reverse gears – the gears allowing it to be driven through the box in one direction and then, by the driver moving his position, back in the opposite direction.

Early in the 1930s, Finland's first commercial vehicle manufacturer emerged – the Sisu company – and in Italy the famous Alfa Romeo company launched into truck manufacture. It is an interesting point that the Alfa Romeo diesel truck designs of the 1930s were, with apparently little modification, taken up after World War II in Brasil where they were produced until 1975 as FNs by Fabrica Nacional de Motores whose manufacturing activities are now controlled by Fiat.

Apart from the already large Mitsubishi and Isuzu developments in Japan, there were other of today's giants moving into the truck world, notably (in 1931) Mazda, with small, three-wheeled load carriers, and Toyota, with its model Gl truck in 1936. Few people, even in Japan, would have believed then in a prophecy that forty years on the Japanese motor industry would become the world's biggest exporter.

Left: a jeep leads an American column of GMCs winding its way into Germany

CHAPTER 4

Back to the Front

As war clouds gathered in Europe in 1939, governments looked at the truck makers to gauge their war potential, not just for road and on-and-off-highway vehicles but armoured fighting machines. In Britain, eyes turned particularly to Leyland with the result that work was put in hand on a new 'secret' factory at Farington for the production of tanks. When built, this brand new red brick structure was given the code name 'BX'. It was not, apparently, a secret to the enemy and Leyland wryly recalls that before it could even be given its coat of camouflage paint it fell victim to a German daylight bombing raid. Leyland also comments that it was later found that the Luftwaffe maps pinpointed the factory, the company somewhat naiively indicating that this emphasised the importance that the German air force placed on Leyland's war potential. This was, of course, hardly surprising, for Leyland's World War I effort had been formidable and it was now a giant organisation compared with those days.

As a truck producer, Leyland's immediate reaction to the outbreak of war was to evolve a three-point programme to meet government requirements. As a result, there was an immediate increase in output of specialised government vehicles already on order. Certain classes of commercial goods vehicles were adapted for service with the armed forces and the diesel engine production for Matilda tanks was stepped up along with the plans to build the tanks themselves.

Production of several general service type 6 × 4 Retriever trucks was increased to fifty a week and work on the Hippo heavy six-wheeler pushed hard; a prototype four-wheeler, the Lynx, was also put forward for trial. Leyland's contribution to Britain's effort in this war was, however, to be less in truck manufacture than tanks, which on the face of it were not Leyland's forte: it was not a munitions company at all. Production of diesel engines for tanks however, eventually led in 1943 to Leyland accepting design responsibility for Centaur and Cromwell tanks and then Comets. This last model was an all-welded design with an entirely new 77mm gun, and it was this tank used by the 11th Armoured Division which spearheaded the final drive into Germany. Also, like numerous other truck builders in wartime, Leyland also switched part of its resources to other war material, particularly high explosive bombs, incendiaries and shells.

Britain's truck industry in the first years of the war was a major target for German bombers, which had their successes. General Motors' British factories, for instance, did not go unscathed. What is now an AC Delco factory of General Motors at Southampton was originally leased in 1938 for the assembly of army trucks. On 30 November 1940, practically the whole factory was destroyed in a single raid. This did not deter the workforce and, by March 1941, the plant was assembling trucks at the rate of over thirty a week – out of doors in fine weather and in an open-sided shed when it was snowing. When the war was over, the factory went back into civilian life by repairing and servicing army trucks for sale on the civilian market, an experience typical of the many plants hit by the German bombers.

Later in the war, of course, the boot was on the other foot and it is difficult to imagine how truck production ever started again in factories like the MAN works in Munich which was absolutely devastated by Allied air attacks. That they did, speaks well of the German industry's resilience.

One lesson learned from World War I and the years afterwards was that there were entirely different requirements for military vehicles from those used for commercial purposes. A rugged chassis was a prerequisite with no question of paring down weight to boost payload, for payload was not the overriding factor. What was needed was an ability to negotiate the most difficult types of terrain. This normally meant an all-wheel-drive capability, or – in multi-wheelers – at least a 6 × 4 configuration and a chassis sufficiently high to avoid ground obstructions. Road tyres were not a practical proposition, high flotation cross-country tyres being the natural choice. This design was specified by everyone, and the USA, for example, made a particular point of all-wheel drive capability when laying down their military vehicle specifications in the 1930s.

The Germans were particularly stringent in setting out their requirements with distinct dividing lines – light, medium and heavy – in the vehicles prescribed. Not that the impact of this was as great as it might have been for, within eighteen months of hostilities starting, the Germans were able to put into service thousands of vehicles captured from the Belgians, Dutch, French and British. They also had the manufacturing facilities of the Czechoslovakian factories of companies like Skoda and Tatra. In the same way, of course, numerous Italian and German vehicles captured by the British in North Africa were put to equally good use.

The measures taken by Leyland at the outbreak of war reflected the fact that not everyone in Britain in 1939 was blind to a breakout of hostilities, and another British manufacturer was perhaps even more prepared for war: Guy Motors Government contracts in the mid and late 1930s had led Guy into dropping commercial vehicle production to specialise in Government work. In the early part of the decade, Guy developed an all-wheel-drive military eight-wheeler, which was in widespread use, and also the Quad Ant, a light four-wheel-drive truck. This was a versatile vehicle and such were the wartime needs of civilian operators that in 1941 a civilian version, the Vixen, was produced from it. As a development of the four-wheel-drive Guy Quad Ant, the company produced the first British rear-engined four-wheel-drive armoured car featuring welded construction of armour plate. This was a real technical breakthrough as, until this time, it had not been thought feasible. The advantages of welded construction were a considerable reduction in the numbers of casualties from 'splash' and rivet heads flying around inside vehicles when hit, a substantial saving (around £100 million) in production costs and, because the concept provided a waterproofing, vehicles were able to wade to a considerable depth. It was this advance in welding which was incorporated in the Comet Tank. Wading ability turned out to be a major requirement for vehicles in the war and, of course, this was taken a great deal further in amphibious vehicle development.

The first really successful amphibian was probably that of the German Hans Trippel in the 1930s, although obviously there had been many previous attempts to make such machines going back to the days of Oliver Evans in the early 1800s. Trippel's amphibians in the war were

Right: various German light trucks crossing a tributary of the Oise at Senlis near Paris

Below: German motorised infantry on the move using half-track outfits built by Mercedes-Benz and powered by Maybach V12, 185bhp units

ANOTHER EXAMPLE OF WHAT A BETTER TRUCK CAN DO

Building the Ramparts as we Watch

America is secure against any wave of the future pounding at her shores . . . as long as there are men and machines to build America's ramparts stronger, faster and better than is possible anywhere else in the world.

The U. S. Army's tremendous new Ravenna Ordnance Arsenal, now under construction, is typical of the many huge defense projects which White Super Power Trucks are helping speed to completion.

Your truck requirements may not *test* the superlative performance and dependability that make White Trucks the acknowledged leader on projects of this magnitude, but your business can *profit* from the extra earning power their reserve of performance and dependability makes possible.

White

THE WHITE MOTOR COMPANY, CLEVELAND
Builders of the complete line of White Super Power Trucks, city and inter-city coaches, Safety School Busses and the famous White Horse.

FOR 40 YEARS THE GREATEST NAME IN TRUCKS

ANOTHER EXAMPLE OF WHAT A BETTER TRUCK CAN DO

Trucks You Don't Steer...You Aim

The shortest distance between two points is a straight line, but roads seldom run that way. To the mechanized cavalry of the U. S. Army, this meant just one thing . . . design and build armored vehicles that can leave the traveled road almost anywhere enroute and not by A. W. O. L. when the engagement begins.

A dry river bed or a route through a stone quarry could be preferable to U. S. Route 1. The result: the Government's order for more than 2500 White Scout Cars has been completed five months ahead of schedule. White Super Power Half-Track . . . trucks that you can steer and easily, but if necessary you can aim over the roughest terrain-men can ride over . . . are rolling off the production line and soon 5,000 will be added to the Army's mechanized forces. As in all commercial fields, White quality makes it possible to rely on transportation equipment to do unusual jobs unusually well.

THE WHITE MOTOR COMPANY, Cleveland
Builders of the complete line of White Super Power Trucks, city and inter-city coaches, Safety School Busses and the Famous White Horse

White

FOR 40 YEARS THE GREATEST NAME IN TRUCKS

Below: one of the most successful amphibious load carriers of World War II was the ubiquitous 'Duck' or the DUKW to give it its full title, operated by the US Army. Built by GMC, they were powered by 104bhp, six-cylinder engines

Left: the White Motor Company of Cleveland emphasised its war effort in its publicity, producing these advertisiements for home consumption

personnel carriers rather than trucks, however, and the same goes for the Schwimmwagens produced by Porsche and Volkswagen. The nearest to a goods carrier – and it was certainly used extensively for this purpose – was the DUKW, or Duck (as it became affectionately called), a six-wheel-drive vehicle built by the American company of Sparkman and Stevens on a GMC truck chassis. Over 20,000 of these went into service in the war, and they had one very unusual feature at that time – the ability to vary tyre pressure while on the move to suit the terrain.

Probably the most well known conventional army trucks in the British forces in the war were those produced by Vauxhall Motors. Vauxhall built ¾ ton and 3 ton army trucks on a vast scale to the British Government's demands for 1000 vehicles a week. Anyone who

Right: Morris Commerical gun tractors of of the 8th Army advance on Gabes, Tunisia, in 1943; a restored Morris tractor is seen below. They were powered by 3·52-litre, four-cylinder engines which produced 70bhp at 3000rpm. Early versions, like the restored vehicle, had permanent four-wheel drive

served in the armed forces in World War II will appreciate Vauxhall's comment that it became virtually the standard British army lorry. Their reliability, simplicity and versatility gave them a very healthy reputation, and they were in great demand for commercial haulage after the war as a result.

Morris and Austin were names which came into army truck production in a big way in the war period with 1 ton 4 × 4s and 3-tonners; Austin also produced a 6 × 6. The successful development of both companies in post-war years in the light and medium-weight truck markets owes much to the volume production of the war period.

Two other names prominent with the British armed forces were those of Commer and Karrier, which had linked up in 1934 within the Rootes Group. Five years of consolidation had followed that event and then came the war, a period in which Commer built 20,000 trucks and Karrier 10,000. In addition, armoured cars, six-wheelers and 4 × 4s, streamed from the Luton works.

Other vehicles built by Ford and Chevrolet in Britain and Canada – and very much like the military (bonneted) Austins, Morrises and Commers – formed the main British military truck park although names like Thornycroft, Dennis, Crossley, Maudslay and Foden were

also well in evidence. It is significant that the majority of these concerns were heavy vehicle makers and it is relevant that, like Leyland, they switched largely to tank production, particularly Dennis and Foden.

A make which was to become particularly well remembered for its role in the war was Scammell. This company points out that, without doubt, the best-known wartime Scammell was that developed from its pre-war heavy duty tractor, the Pioneer. This was a heavy breakdown recovery tractor, 2235 of which were supplied during the war; Scammell also produced 548 tank transporters.

Use by the British (and later the US) forces of road transporters for moving tanks was in marked contrast to the German method in the first years of the conflict. The Germans relied on rail for movement over long distances and then on direct overland movement. This resulted in higher wear rates and breakdowns on German tanks than on the Allied units, especially on the Russian front. Although rather later the Germans seem to have realised the merits of tank transporters, there is little doubt that in the middle years of the war their effort was adversely affected by the lack of them.

Development of tank transporters also had a marked impact on road transport for the construction industry after hostilities ended. Most tank transporters were based on the principle of the semi-trailer, having a knock-out back axle which, when removed, allowed the tank to be driven on to the load deck before the axles were re-attached. After the war such vehicles were in widespread demand to move bulldozers and other large items of construction plant to meet the needs of rebuilding ravaged towns and cities.

There were, of course, infinite variations on the commercial vehicle theme with articulated vehicles. One of the most common sights in Britain during the war was that of Bedford tractor units hauling sixty foot long trailers carrying fuselages for aircraft such as Spitfires and Hurricanes, along with aircraft wings and other components. These 'Queen Marys', as they were affectionately dubbed, were used extensively in post-war years for aircraft movement. Their surprisingly low hauling capability of 6 tons did not prevent their Bedford motive units from being used effectively for hauling all kinds of purpose-built trailers equipped with special racking for carrying bombs, shells and torpedoes.

It was not this model which was to make GMCs name in the war, however, although, like its British Vauxhall subsidiary across the Atlantic, GMC established itself as the leading US military truck supplier. The company did this with its bonneted 6 × 6s, building an incredible 600,000 in the war period, all fitted with what it called the 'Army Workhorse Engine', a six-cylinder power unit producing 104 bhp.

One of the main suppliers of trucks to the US forces was the Marmon-Harrington organisation of Indianapolis which specialised in 4 × 4 and 6 × 6 units; this company also handled all-wheel-drive conversion work for bigger manufacturers like Ford. FWD itself, of course, came strongly into the picture in the case of vehicles driving on all wheels, supplying its own 4 × 4, 6-tonner with a Waukesha engine.

Autocar, Diamond T, White, Reo, Kenworth and Oshkosh were all very much in the 6 × 6, 6-ton truck making business and their wartime legacy of military vehicles is in evidence even now in many parts of the world. There are, for instance, still quite a few ex-wartime Diamond T vehicles (usually converted to recovery vehicles) operational in Europe.

In design terms probably one of the few long-term contributions to truck design came from Willys with its ubiquitous Jeep. After the war the light 4 × 4 concept established by this concern was accepted worldwide as the right formula for light goods carriers in all types of construction work and off-highway situations.

In France, as Berliet recalls, war and the Occupation reduced activity and that company concentrated its efforts on the construction of *gazobois* trucks using wood as fuel. It was the same with the majority of other French manufacturers like Renault, Latil, Somua and Saviem; development stagnated. During the Occupation, of course, the main French factories were forced to supply vehicles for the German armed forces, but production was at a much lower level than in the years leading up to the conflict.

In retrospect, it is obvious that Occupation hit the French industry harder than any other in Europe. There was little in the way of design progress until the 1950s when the French went ahead in the development of front-wheel-drive designs. The Citroën model H, with its semi-forward control layout, was to become a familiar sight in French towns. It offered a low-load platform height of 19in, thus satisfying an increasingly important factor in delivery vehicle selection. There was, however, one very notable French contribution to the advancement of truck design and this came from Michelin. In 1947, the French tyre giant started developing the steel radial tyre which was to raise payloads and result in extensive operating economies for the heavy vehicle operating industry.

Another major development in the French industry of the 1950s was the merger of Somua, Latil and the heavy vehicle division of Renault

Above right: a convoy of Morris Commercial 8cwt PV four-wheel-drive personnel-carrier trucks and Austin troop carriers seen in Belgium in May 1940

Right: a row of Chevrolet trucks on their way to the Burma Road

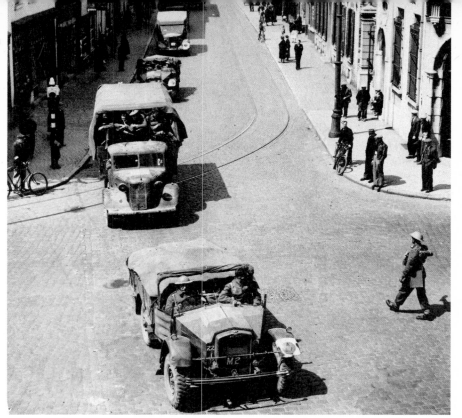

into Saviem (Société Anonyme de Véhicles Industriels et d'Equipements Mécaniques). This became Renault's heavy vehicle organisation in 1959 as a result of Renault becoming a majority shareholder – a move which can be seen as the foundation of what is today (with Berliet) the hard core of the French truck-making industry.

The preparedness of the German forces for war in 1939 was reflected in the high mobility of the German army. Their use of motorised infantry, employing purpose-built trucks in particular, was in marked relief to the Polish and even the French forces which still had a high proportion of horse-drawn equipment. Transport men in Britain were staggered in 1939 at seeing newspaper photographs of French troops moving to the front with guns hauled by teams of horses.

This German mobility was due in no small measure to the Schell Programme of 1938 which organised military lorry production on a highly planned basis, often to a uniform specification by several manufacturers; road vehicles fell into lightweight, middleweight and heavyweight categories in a scale of five classes of weights from 1 ton to $6\frac{1}{2}$ tons payload and with engines of no less than a defined minimum power output.

This policy can be seen as one of the main long-term influences on German truck design because it established the principle of minimum power-to-weight ratios for trucks. A requirement of less than 8bhp per ton of a vehicle's gross weight ensured in the German truck boom of the 1950s and 1960s that vehicles were not underpowered.

The active German Manufacturers in the war were Borgward,

Below: trucks were adapted for all sorts of work in the war – here one is carrying sections of a pontoon bridge. This truck is an Albion BY3 3 ton 6 x 4, which was powered by a six-cylinder 80bhp engine; it was in production from 1940 to 1941

Below right: a German half track towing a 150cm gun, is watched by locals as it enters Russian territory. The outfit is a Maybach-powered Krauss-Maffei built in 1934; power output is 115bhp and payload is 8 tons

Bottom right: local carpenters in India are quickly adapting these local vehicles for war work

Daimler-Benz, Magirus, Hanomag, Büssing, Opel, the German Ford organisation, Krupp, MAN, Henschel and Faun. Austrian producers like OAF, Steyr and Austro-Daimler should be added to this list along with the Czechoslovak producers. An interesting point about all German vehicles of this period is that they were all bonneted units and fitted diesel engines almost exclusively in the heavier weight classes. Like the British – as opposed to the US manufacturers – they produced a mixture of 4×2, 4×4, 6×2, 6×4 and 6×6 designs.

Some of the vehicles had unusual design features. The Daimler-Benz lightweight, for instance, had air-cooled petrol engines. Air-cooled

Deutz diesels were fitted in a number of makes, including Magirus and Henschel, whilst Tatra's 6 × 6 design had a big, eight-cylinder, air-cooled petrol engine. A light air-cooled diesel was produced for North African use with special air filtration to check dust ingress. Henschel produced a 6 × 6, 6½-tonner which was designed so that it could be adapted for use on rail. Büssing, which had acquired the NAG concern of Berlin in 1931, had a six-wheeled cross-country vehicle, developed by NAG, which could have special tracks fitted over the tyres of its rear bogie, effectively turning it into a half track.

This was one of the more successful vehicles to be used on the Russian front, which generated the requirements for an entirely different type of vehicle. Lack of roads comparable with those of Western Europe meant rough surfaces which played havoc with pneumatic-tyred vehicles; half tracks were ideal for such conditions.

As in Britain and the USA, so in Germany, traditional truck producers like MAN turned part of their manufacturing resources over to tank production, but for others, like Krupp, truck production was only a small part of the war effort compared with munitions.

Italy's Fiat had produced a six-wheeled forward control truck in 1936 called the Dovunque 35 and this, with the light TL 37 pick-up truck,

produced in 1937, plus the 626N and CL 39 (both forward control four-wheelers), provided the bulk of the Italian army's vehicle fleet. When Italy entered the war, in 1941, the T 40, again a forward control four-wheeler, was introduced and, two years after that, the Dovunque 41 – a forward control six-wheeler of a very modern design and concept.

Both the German and the Italian industries suffered heavily in air raids in the war, some like Büssing's NAG factory in Berlin being totally obliterated by the bombing and Russian gunfire. The Fiat works in Turin were hit very hard by huge raids in the summer of 1943 and, in fact, no German truck factory was left untouched in the last two years of the war by RAF and US Air Force bombing.

Such were the air attacks on German truck factories in 1944 and 1945 that there was hardly a production line left in operation. Daimler-Benz recalls the words of the company's board in 1945 that, 'when the Second World War ended, Daimler-Benz had practically ceased to exist'.

However, rebuilding started at once, for there was a pressing need for trucks, and out of it all came a new all-purpose vehicle which (in much refined form) has been produced right up to the present day. This was the Unimog. Launched in 1946 as an all-wheel-drive, high clearance, 1-ton load carrier, it incorporated many of the lessons learned from military experience of the needs of vehicles engaged in on-and-off-highway work.

Such was the speed of Daimler-Benz's recuperation that by 1951 annual car and commercial vehicle production had reached 42,000 units; by 1961, output was almost 200,000 and in 1971 almost 500,000.

Post-war recovery at Magirus Deutz led, in 1948, to the series production of air-cooled diesel engines for light and medium-weight vehicles and then, in 1951, to a major development – the debut at the Frankfurt Motor Show of the company's 170 hp, air-cooled, V8 diesel in a maximum capacity truck. After a period of manufacturing re-organisation, a 250 hp, air-cooled, V12 diesel followed in 1955. This range of air-cooled vee engines – with refinements, of course – is fitted today throughout the Magirus range.

If the rest of the European truck industry had not actually ground to a halt in 1945, it was nevertheless in a bad way in many countries. Fiat recalls that the number of commercial vehicles in circulation in Italy in 1945 was badly depleted and quite inadequate for the country's needs, most vehicles being war relics. Along with companies like Alfa Romeo and Lancia, Fiat set to work to build trucks again in order to expand road transport and so aid the economy. As a result, a whole new range of light, medium and heavy trucks was built in the period from 1948 to 1951, being completed in 1952 with the 682N 8tons load capacity model. Fiat says that this can be considered as the base upon which later models were designed. It is interesting that, with the exception of one light truck model, this and all subsequent on-highway Fiat vehicles have been built on the forward control principle.

Britain's truck industry too had been hit hard by air raids in the early years of the war but was less and less affected as it progressed. As a result, the British industry was in a better position than those of the rest of Europe in the immediate post-war era.

They exploited their advantage. The Rootes Group, for example, continued with the bonneted Superpoise range, first launched in 1939, and in 1948 produced a model with an under-floor engine. Karrier, in the same year, redesigned its purpose-built, stop-start, 2-ton delivery vehicle, the Bantam, and supplemented it with a bigger 3/4-ton outfit, the Gamecock, in 1950. By 1953, the company was producing vehicles at a level 215 per cent up on 1938/39 and, as a result – as part of a policy of expansion – a £1,000,000 factory (at that time a very big investment)

was established in Dunstable. Ex-wartime Bedford trucks converted for civilian use were in great demand in the post-war period but it was nonetheless realised that they were 'a bit short on payload'. As a result, at London's Earls Court Show in 1950, Vauxhall unveiled its 'Big Bedford' range of models, fitted with a 4·9-litre, six-cylinder petrol engine which many operators regarded as the best commercial vehicle petrol engine, regardless of its price, in its size range.

Nevertheless, when a company moved up the weight scale, diesel engines were needed, and Vauxhall for instance fitted the first of its own design of 3·4 and 4·8 litres capacity in 1957, Perkins and Leyland engines having been optionally available until this time.

As the world's biggest exporters in the early 1960s, the influence of British manufacturers was very strong. For example, the Finnish Sis and Vanaja concerns fitted Leyland and AEC diesels, respectively, in this period and used a great deal of the expertise of these companies.

The know-how of the same two companies was used by other European concerns, notably the Dutch company DAF which used Leyland engines extensively in its vehicles. There were, too, any number of small Dutch and Belgian concerns which used AEC engines (as alternatives to Gardners) and components in a variety of on-and-off highway vehicles. In Britain, the Dodge company at Kew had a huge output from a tiny factory achieved on the strength of using bought-in components and notably AEC diesel engines.

AEC was a far-sighted company and it was realised in the 1950s that a stake in truck-building was needed on the European mainland. As a result, AEC in 1962, took a controlling interest in the French Willème concern. Although this period of ownership continued through to British Leyland's acquisition of AEC in 1964 and beyond to the 1970s, it never seemed to make the advance originally envisaged with the result that it quietly disappeared as a manufacturing force.

In Britain and Europe, a characteristic of the late 1940s and early 'fifties was that production materials were in very short supply. This led to experiments with new materials and the use of glassfibre for such items as body panels, wings, bonnets, transmission covers and even for complete cabs became commonplace, especially in Britain where the smaller manufacturers like Seddon, ERF and Scammell made extensive use of this material.

Foden recalls that in three years no vehicle could be sold on the home market unless a similar one was shipped overseas, so Foden – along with other British manufacturers, incidentally – concentrated, with considerable success, on markets in the Commonwealth, particularly the Rhodesias, South Africa and Australia.

The post-war years saw the disappearance, on take-over or merger, of many famous names. AEC was the first to go on the takeover trail in Britain after the war, Crossley being acquired in 1948 and Maudslay the following year.

Then came the turn of Leyland, who acquired the Scottish firm of Albion Motors in 1951 and then Scammell Lorries in 1955. Both companies retained their own identity and models for some 20 years after their respective acquisitions and, in fact, the Scammell name still survived in 1978.

The wartime efforts of both the Austin and Morris companies were continued after 1945, with both companies consolidating on the success of their wartime designs in the light and medium-weight spheres, although Austin introduced a revised range in 1950. However, it seemed a logical move, in 1952, for these companies to merge their similar interests to form the British Motor Corporation. Main results of the merger were rationalisation of designs and the introduction, in 1954, of a range of diesel engines ranging in size from 2·1 to 5·1 litres.

Guy Motors turned from fighting vehicle to truck production, concentrating initially on its Vixen, Wolf and other models in the 2 to 6 tons markets. However, in 1954 it re-entered the heavy vehicle market with its Big Otter and Invincible ranges and, later, its Warrior models. Guy was not, however, to survive long into the 1960s as an independent company, being acquired by the Jaguar car concern in 1961.

After the takeover by Jaguar, Guy engineers went to work on what was to be the company's most successful post-war range. Called the Guy Big J, it was launched in 1964 and was produced steadily thereafter for more than ten years. It was also to be Guy's swan song, for the name disappeared when its production ceased in 1975 and the factory turned to other Leyland Products, Jaguar having become part of the British Leyland Group in 1966.

A suprising small vehicle fleet was operated by the Japanese in the war in the Far East and it was, of course, in the post-war era that the Japanese laid the foundations of what is today, numerically, the world's biggest truck exporting industry.

As early as 1946, Hino Motors built Japan's first 15-ton articulated outfit which was followed in 1947 by an air-braked, articulated bus. Volume manufacture of large diesel trucks and buses came in 1949 and in 1951 the company added a 6×6, 10-ton truck, built for construction work. This was significant for it marked the step into this sector which was to be carried on with a heavy dumper model in 1954. Hino claims to have introduced Japan's first twin steering 6×2 in 1958.

Japanese manufacturers entered into agreements with a number of European concerns, for example Datsun for a while used Renault expertise and Isuzu Motors linked with Rootes for technological

assistance, an arrangement which ceased on the latter's acquisition by Chrysler in the 1960s.

Mitsubishi Motors Corporation, part of the group that had played such a big part in supplying the Japanese war machine with equipment, moved into gear on the commercial scene in 1946 with the production of three-wheeled trucks and heavy duty buses. Similarly, in the same year, Nissan Diesel resumed production of civilian trucks and buses and eventually, in 1955, started a major expansion programme by introducing 5-ton, 7½-ton and 10½-ton trucks powered respectively by 130bhp, 150bhp and 230bhp two-stroke diesel engines.

Nissan Motor Co started light truck production under the Datsun name with pick-ups in 1947, concentrating throughout the 1950s on this class of vehicle. Toyo Kogyo, manufacturing under the Mazda name, started in light truck production in 1950, rather later than Nissan, and they specialised in this type of vehicle during the 'fifties. Toyota at that time followed a similar pattern, concentrating on car production.

Right: a wood-burning Volvo of the World War II period. The ability to run without precious liquid fuel kept many civilian vehicles on the road during the war years

Below right: a gunner watches for an air attack as an American column advances to the north of France. The vehicle is a 6 × 6 GMC CCKW-352 which was powered by a six-cylinder, 104bhp engine

Bottom: row upon row of Ford 1½-ton 2G8T vehicles await shipping to the front lines

The American industry in the immediate post-war days returned to civilian truck production with particular zest. Their industry, in the world sense, was cock of the walk. American trucks had become universally popular and manufacturers couldn't build enough new ones to meet world demand.

This was the heyday of US truck exports – take a look at the figures: in 1947, the US industry shipped 267,379 trucks overseas and 204,831 in the following year. Britain was second biggest exporter with 48,783 and 73,996 in the same years which demonstrates the extent of the American lead.

It was also to be the era of the 'West Coast type' of heavy duty tractor unit for hauling articulated trailers – a design trend which shaped the pattern for hauling 35-ton loads over long distances, not only in the USA, but worldwide.

The US industry was full of ideas and had the expertise to back them. With lessons learned from the aircraft industry, aluminium alloy was gradually coming into use in body construction. That chassis manufacturers also built the bodies was now accepted and the big companies, where they had not already done so, expanded into this field. International Harvester recalls, for example, that in 1948 the company acquired, as a subsidiary, the Metropolitan Body Company at Bridgeport, Connecticut, which for a number of years previously had manufactured the bodies for International Harvester's Metro delivery trucks.

The first monocoque-bodies trucks made their debut in the immediate post-war years, first with light passenger-car-based vehicles, then with purpose-built commercial vehicle designs.

Probably the most significant trend of all in the post-war era, in terms of world impact on road transport, was the shift to articulated vehicle operations for virtually all heavy duty road work. The move was strongest in the USA and in Britain. It was less widespread on the European mainland where, in Germany and Italy in particular, the main workhorse was still the lorry and drawbar trailer. The impact of this move to articulation was felt in the late 1950s when trailer design principles developed by such companies as Fruehauf and Highway crossed the Atlantic and were used extensively under licence agreements.

In the USA, articulation had been taken a stage further. Use of double bottom (a tractor unit hauling two semi-trailers) had become a fact of life – particularly on the West Coast routes. The normal outfit took two 22ft long semi-trailers which resulted in an overall vehicle train length of around 55ft, although there were some much longer combinations in operation. This type of operation has only recently (in the 1970s) attracted interest in Europe; lack of appeal for such outfits has stemmed from the fact that they have been illegal under the construction and use laws of most European countries, although their experimental use is now being allowed, by special dispensation, in some instances.

A new dimension to articulated vehicle use was added in the 1950s when forward control tilt cabs started to be fitted in quantity on big tractor units in the USA. In the preceding decade, the merits of forward control on artic tractor units had become generally recognised as offering the possibility of hauling longer trailers with greater payloads, the overall aim being a 35ft deck length within a 45ft overall combination length. The problem then was in allowing good engine access for repairs and maintenance. Tilting the cab on forward-mounted pivot points provided the answer and all the big companies like Mack, International Harvester, Ford, General Motors and White introduced tilt-cab designs, although Diamond T is believed to be the first successful producer.

This move to tilt cabs was not followed in Europe until the 1960s, although, strangely enough, forward control was accepted to a much greater degree.

CHAPTER 5

Applied Technology

In truck manufacture, the heart of the vehicle is its engine, and its performance is frequently the key to success or failure of a particular model. Preoccupation with the power pack has accordingly been a keynote of the truck since it first appeared on the roads, but in recent years environmental considerations and the world oil situation have imposed new dimensions on powering vehicles. The past thirty years in truck development has seen the automotive diesel replace the petrol engine in almost every sphere of the truck market. Quite a number of the diesel engines in use in the post-war era were of the pre-combustion chamber type, and it was not until the late 1940s and early 1950s that direct injection took over completely, reflecting the start of post-war development in diesel design.

In Britain, two two-stroke designs were of particular interest. It was in 1948 that Foden exhibited its four-cylinder two stroke at the London Commercial Motor Show, while the second major development was by the Rootes Group in 1955. Their unusual three-cylinder unit with its particularly distinctive engine note turned out to be very successful in both diesel and multi-fuel versions, and was in use in Rootes Group medium-weight trucks until the late 1960s. In the USA, General Motors two-stroke diesels were so successful that the range was continually improved, and expanded to the point where today it is undoubtedly the world's most successful two-stroke diesel. However, most makers relied on four-cycle, four and six-cylinder in-line designs.

It was in the 1950s that turbocharging of truck diesel engines became accepted – at least by some manufacturers – and, as a concept, its development owes much to Volvo. In the 1950s, the continually increasing gross laden weight of trucks (Sweden, incidentally is allowed the biggest road outfits in the world) made necessary higher and higher engine outputs. Many manufacturers chose to build larger and larger engines, but this created problems, and they were not only heavy but required a large amount of installation space; they also consumed a lot of fuel. Volvo chose to supercharge by turbo-compressor to get more power from smaller engines where engine output could be increased by up to 50% with the same swept volume and only a slight increase in weight. A more complete combustion could be achieved, and this resulted in lower fuel consumption, quieter running and unchanged output at high altitudes. As a result, the Volvo L395, introduced in 1954, was the first successful truck with a turbocharged diesel engine. It was a concept which was to receive slow but ever-increasing support until today it is widespread.

Left: a world away from the draughty, slow and cramped trucks of the early days. An International Transtar forward-control outfit eases its way across the American continent in the late 1970s

The 1950s saw American diesel-engine development start to move ahead in great leaps in the heavy vehicle classes, although it was not for another ten years that the main conversion from petrol engines occurred. As early as 1953, Mack announced its Thermodyne diesel (high torque output) which was to be attractive to the operator of maximum capacity articulated outfits.

US manufacturers awakened to the benefits of diesel economy in delivery vehicles in the early 1960s, and there was a boom market for imported diesels. The company which benefitted most, perhaps, was the British Perkins company which enjoyed a several hundred per cent expansion in engine sales particularly of its 6·354 diesel engine design. This, for example, was offered widely by Chrysler from 1963 onwards in its Dodge middleweight trucks built for city and suburban goods delivering services.

Cummins diesels steadily increased in popularity as the reliability of the company's in-line six-cylinder design steadily improved. The company recalls that up to the mid 1950s, it had been a one-plant,

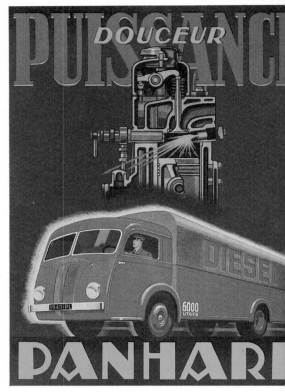

one product company, but was now looking to international expansion. In 1956, it set up a manufacturing plant in Scotland, not far from the Euclid (later Terex) plant of General Motors (Euclid having been acquired by GM in 1954), to whom it was a main engine supplier.

High-speed vee diesels made their debut in the early 1960s, with Cummins announcing in 1961 two 90° V6 and V8 designs, the V6 200 and the V8 265, the numbers indicating the bhp output. It was with these engines that Cummins mounted its real assault on the European market, signing agreements with Jaguar in Britain and Krupp in Germany, to manufacture under the Jaguar-Cummins and Krupp-Cummins names. Later, a further agreement was entered into, this time with Chrysler, to produce two further lightweight V6 and V8 high-speed diesels of 185 and 200bhp, respectively. These ventures were doomed to failure and all the partnerships were dissolved. The smaller V6 and V8 engines, after early set-backs, are now produced in improved form in quantity for world markets at Cummins's Darlington, England, manufacturing plants.

Other manufacturers were looking to vee-configuration diesels in the 1960s, and in January 1964 GMC introduced the Toro-Flow, a 60° four-stroke engine for middle-weight trucks producing maximum power at 3200rpm.

Like the Cummins designs, however, other vee-engines got off to a poor start and AEC's experience with a powerful V8 unit produced in the late 1960s was so unfortunate that it was withdrawn from production altogether. There have also been successes, notably that of the Scania V8

and of the Mercedes V10 engines, which power the company's 1977 heavy duty ranges. On air-cooled diesels, turbocharging by the main automotive producer Magirus Deutz was not tried until 1972 when two versions of the company's V12 design were fitted with turbochargers to produce 500 and 1000bhp, respectively, for off-highway dump truck rather than road vehicle application.

A tremendous flurry of interest in automotive gas turbines occurred in the late 1960s. American vehicle manufacturers were well ahead, with prototype turbine-engine trucks and dumpers, built by at least five vehicle manufacturers, running in proving service. They were the Chrysler Corporation, the Ford Motor Co, Mack Trucks, the Detroit Diesel Engine division of General Motors and the Solar division of International Harvester. In fact, some of the companies produced vehicle prototypes with turbine engines as far back as the early 1950s. Of these designs, probably the most spectacular was the giant Lectra Haul M100, 100-ton load capacity dumper manufactured by the Unit Rig and Equipment Company of Tulsa, but powered by a 1100bhp Saturn gas turbine built by the Solar division of the International Harvester Company. In Europe, Leyland announced a gas turbine powered truck in 1968, and claimed to be in the lead in development having had many years of experiment, including the fitting of a gas turbine in a Rover car which competed at Le Mans. Magirus Deutz was the first manufacturer to produce a gas turbine engined truck in Germany. Also announced in 1968, the power unit had an output similar to the Leyland – 250 to 450bhp. Ten years later, gas turbine powered trucks have not really got off the ground, and few people consider they have a role in the truck world of the future.

Road development was an increasing influence on European truck development in the 1960s with, strangely at first sight, the construction of the Asian highway, linking the Middle East with India and the Far East by way of Afghanistan, probably having the most powerful influence. In the 1970s, the opening up of through-road transport services from Western Europe to Iran, Afghanistan and India were made possible by this development.

Motorway construction everywhere created a need not only for larger, more powerful engines and transmissions built for long-distance, high-speed running, but also tyres which stood up to this class of work. Fortunately, the industry met the challenge, but it took rather longer to improve braking standards. Vacuum brakes, where used, were steadily supplemented by air brake systems in the heavier vehicle ranges with air/hydraulic units taking over in the intermediate weight classes. As vehicle gross weights increased, at-the-wheels braking systems started to be supplemented increasingly by exhaust brakes and later retarders, engine-retarders of the US-designed Jacobs type vieing with the electro-mechanical unit of the type popularised by the French Telma company.

There were quite a few important steps in truck transmission development in the post-war years. Synchronised gearing was introduced by many manufacturers in the late 1940s and 1950s and, rather later in the 1950s, range change and splitter boxes and two-speed back axles appeared on the scene.

Air suspension, developed in the USA by leading rubber companies like Firestone, was tried extensively on commercial vehicles with varying degrees of success in the 1950s, although the main application was to buses and coaches where practically every leading world manufacturer developed designs. Perhaps predictably, the American industry was well in the lead on air suspension at this time, although European concerns like Dunlop were making a real impression in the late 1950s. Since then, of course, air suspension has become accepted in a wide

Below : a 1953 poster advertising 'America's toughest truck' the Reo. Would other manufacturers have disagreed?

Bottom: looking a world apart from the Reo just five years its junior is this 1958 Mack Model N

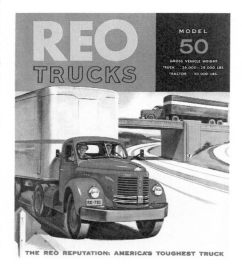

Left: a Peterbilt manufactured in the early 1950s, one of their first 'California Haulers'

Below: an early application of the turbine/electric principle on an International Solar powered Lectra Haul gas-turbine 100 ton tipper; this vehicle has over 1100bhp at its disposal

variety of truck applications, but mainly perhaps in tanker operations and similar usage where smooth riding characteristics are desired. Today, the German MAN concern is probably the leading manufacturer in air suspension, fitting it to a wide variety of the models it produces. Air suspension has also found acceptance in demountable body designs where it can be pumped up and deflated as required to allow bodies on legs to be mounted and demounted from the chassis. This has become sufficiently popular in Germany for Mercedes-Benz to offer the concept as a standard option on both rigid and articulated vehicles. Use of demountable bodies as an alternative to, and simple supplement, articulated vehicle use swept through the world truck industry in the late 1960s and 1970s employing, as alternatives to air, hydraulic and mechanical methods of demounting. Demountable bodies are of course containers and constitute only part of the influence on road transport.

Below left: The kangaroo system was used by the French, Swiss and Italian railways for long-haul trailers. Whether this idea is more practicable than the use of containers is debatable

Below: A GMC 550 semi-trailer outfit

Door-to-door container movement was a topic investigated collectively by the railways of Western Europe in the post-war years as part of the reconstruction of the devastated rail network. Predictably perhaps, there was no far-reaching agreement, with the result that each country tended to pursue its own policies. The French decided to develop the kangaroo system, based on the use of railway wagons purpose-built to take road semi-trailers moving them over long distances. This was to have a formative impact on French truck development, for it reduced the numbers of heavy outfits travelling by road, so that when it came to weight considerations there was virtually no opposition to the thirteen metric ton axle weight limit adopted and still retained by them. This has resulted in truck designs with a minimum number of axles. At one time, in their own countries, a British Leyland or Italian Fiat would have required three or even four-axles to carry the same payload as that which a French Berliet could handle. On the whole, however, the French kangaroo concept is out-of-step with the rest of the world which is geared to freight containers and their easy interchange between different transport modes. The standard ISO freight container with a cross-section of 8ft × 8ft, and in standard lengths of 10ft, 20ft, 30ft and 40ft, has, in fact, proved the biggest single influence on truck design worldwide since the start of 'the container revolution' in the late 1950s and early 1960s.

Use of freight containers was originally a shipping concept, but the ISO module has dictated the standard size of heavy vehicles throughout the world; deck length of 20ft, 30ft and 40ft and a width of rather more than 8ft being the governing dimensions. Maximum permissable weight of containers has also tended to influence maximum vehicle weights, although in some countries, like Britain, environmental considerations have checked uplift in weight limits to a reasonable economic level.

In Britain, however, ISO container use encouraged inter-modal transport thinking, and a brand-new service was established by the railways, the Freightliner concept. This was initially for UK domestic movements only, but now is international. The object of the Freightliner is to exploit high-capacity containers carried on high-speed custom-built rail wagons, running in fixed-formation trains, to provide fast and reliable services over medium and long distances at low cost and with purpose-built container-carrying articulated road vehicles providing the terminal feeder services. The majority of the containers carried meet ISO specifications, so as to make possible the most efficient use of rail/road/sea transport. Containers are accumulated in train-load

quantities at strategically sited terminals throughout the country, and these terminals are specially designed and equipped with purpose-built cranes for the rapid transfer of containers between road and rail or ship, which enables a national integrated door-to-door service.

In Europe, a major formative influence on articulated vehicle design was the TIR carnet agreement signed in the early 1960s to facilitate customs clearance of goods moved internationally by road; the letters TIR stand for Transport International Routier. When shown on a vehicle, they indicate that it complies constructionally with the requirement that the vehicle can be customs-sealed at the beginning of a journey and continue without inspection at frontiers to a foreign destination. This not only cut down the use of open vehicles (which found it difficult to comply with its requirements), but generated the TIR tilt trailer, a sided unit with a specially designed canvas or plastic tilt which could be custom-sealed to enclose the load.

On the rigid vehicle front, a fad for multi-axle units came in the 1960s, and in the USA this took some strange but practical forms. Early in 1965, for example, there was the Reo Tri-Drive, an 8 × 6 normal control design introduced by the Reo Truck Division of the White Motor Co with the aim of carrying considerably more payload than competitive 6 × 4s, yet complying with axle loading requirements. The Hendrickson tri-axle bogie used wide track axles and single low profile tyres which were coming into widespread use of certain classes of work. These fat single tyres were the subject of intensive experiment by fleet operators in the 1960s especially for tanker vehicles and outfits engaged on construction applications. However, as time went by, their limitations were realised with the result that, although used for certain applications, they are not in as widespread use in the 1970s as was

Below: a Fiat Mammut of 1969 with a 30 cubic metre dumping trailer. Note how the tractor has right-hand drive even for the Italian market, where it is thought that the drivers are better off near the outside of the road than the oncoming traffic

Right: a Magirus Deutz 310 waits at a railhead for a container for local deliveries. Magirus have used air-cooled engines for many years, claiming they reach working temperatures quicker, have longer maintenance intervals and, of course, are immune to freezing or boiling

thought likely at the time of their introduction.

The Multi-axle phenomena was not only to be seen in the USA. In Italy, it was particualrly in evidence, but not so much on rigid vehicles as articulated outfits and drawbar trailer rigs. The reason for them was primarily the same as in the USA – axle weight limits. Italy had the lowest axle weight level in Europe at this time – just over 8 tons – yet road trains in certain circumstances were allowed to operate at 44 tons. The result was numerous axles including tracking third axle designs from companies like Ceschi and Viberti. These tracking axles were, later in the 1960s, adopted by several trailer makers in other European countries to spread axle weight and boost payload on maximum capacity articulated vehicle designs where two axle tractors were used.

German legislation in the 1960s not only influenced design on its own territory but elsewhere as well. In 1965, Germany increased its legal maxima for articulated vehicles and lorry and trailer combinations from 32 to 38 metric tons. A 10 ton axle limit and a requirement governing maximum turning circle led, however, to three-axled tractor units being adopted on the heaviest weight outfits along with semi-trailers with tracking axles. As a side issue, it is an interesting point that the first Mercedes-Benz three-axled tractor unit built to meet these new regulations – the LPS 2020 with sleeper cab – was selling at DM 57,500 (then £5040) and that, just over ten years later, the price of the equivalent vehicle was five times that sum, such has been the level of inflation in the countries of Europe.

More firms were merged, taken over and swallowed up in the 1960s. In Britain, Leyland in 1961 acquired Standard-Triumph, and in 1962 there was the really big takeover for Leyland in truck and bus terms.

This was the takeover of Leyland's biggest British rival – Associated Commercial Vehicles, makers of AEC trucks and buses. Then came the absorption of the ailing British Motor Corporation, a move from which Leyland has never recovered. In fact, the once supreme British truck giant has been bled by its car involvement since. Even so, Leyland's truck and bus activities continue to turn in high profit levels.

The American industry slimmed down through takeovers in the 1950s, the White Motor Co being the main company on the move in this connection. Autocar, Diamond T, Reo and Sterling were the companies acquired by White in this period and a notable takeover at that time by Mack was that of Brockway Trucks. The 1960s then saw a period of little change, with the big battalions – Ford, GMC, IH, Mack and Chrysler followed by White – supreme. Then came the custom-builders like Brockway and Kenworth. This is the pattern of the US industry today and a significant point is that these leaders are all international companies. In Europe, in contrast, further mergers and takeovers looked likely.

In Holland, there is the peculiar situation of International Harvester having a substantial stake in the DAF company's truck activities, yet Volvo having a majority interest in the car side but a lesser one in truck production. In Britain, the only sign of the takeover of Seddon-Atkinson by International Harvester in 1975 is the fitment of IH engines in certain models. The acquisition of Seddon-Atkinson left only three independent producers of any note in England – Foden, ERF and Dennis – although the last is owned by a conglomerate and is a very tiny truck maker by modern standards. In France, just Berliet and Saviem are left, but for how much longer is uncertain as a merging of interests is being considered. In 1978, the strong men of Europe are in many ways the Swedish Volvo and Scania companies, where a proposed unification of the two companies has just aborted. Then there is Germany. It was not until the end of the 1960s that the German industry really slimmed down. The Rheinstahl Group was still making Tempo and Vidal vans as was the Hanomag part of its main subsidiary, Hanomag-Henschel. Mercedes-Benz then took over these truck making activities and continued to produce lightweight models to Hanomag's front-wheel-drive designs, but under the Mercedes name. Henschel models, in contrast, gradually phased out so that in 1975 the name disappeared entirely.

Büssing, in the late 1960s, was losing money steadily under the ownership of the Salzgitter Group and in this case MAN stepped in, to continue production of the underfloor-engined vehicle designs and progress the use of air suspension on trucks which Büssing had successfully pioneered. At about this time, too, yet another big name – Krupp – abandoned its truck making activities.

As the 1960s closed, there were the first moves towards co-operation in Europe between companies of different nationalities. MAN, for example, agreed with Saviem to supply the French company with engines and in return fit the Saviem cab on certain models and to market Saviem lightweight models in Germany under the MAN badge.

The progressive easing of customs and other barriers to trade in Europe also created a new concept in tractor units for articulated vehicle work. Most of the major manufacturers are now producing them, and it is worth picking out one at random to illustrate the general concept. The DAF Supercontinental, as it was called, was first produced in 1974, and was built for operation at 50 tonnes, gcw and fitted with a 307bhp diesel engine. Developed for haulage to areas such as North Africa, the Middle East and beyond, it was based on the biggest standard DAF chassis of that time, the FT 2800 DKS. Its principal special feature was the cab, a single berth sleeper unit with living equipment which included a two-ring butane cooker with grill, a stainless steel sink and hand pump,

Left: by the mid 1970s, the rigid eight-wheelers had lost favour completely to the semi-trailer (or artic) outfits, although most manufacturers continued to build them in small numbers. This is a Volvo 8 × 4 F86 model with a 207bhp engine

Far left: a Berliet GHB 12 250bhp six-wheel-drive outfit hauling logs in Nigeria. This type of Berliet is also available in 6 × 4 form

Left: a Scania L50 built at their Brazilian plant in 1974. Note the twelve-wheel trailer

Below: one of the 1970 generation Leylands. This Marathon was designed specially for trans-continental heavy haulage and is powered by a TL12 six-cylinder turbocharged unit

cooled food storage unit, or optional electric refrigerator, 21 gallons of water storage, a small wardrobe unit, a generous storage box and cooking seat (in place of the passenger seat), a 6000 BTU/hour fumeless catalytic heater, two small adjustable electric fans and additional roof vents and interior lights. Externally there was a roof-mounted air conditioning unit and a double skin 'tropical' roof; all glass was laminated and tinted. A full width mesh radiator and light guard were fitted, supplemented – if required – by an optional windscreen guard (also of mesh) and additional spotlights built into the front bumper, an aluminium catwalk behind the cab, a coupling light and lockable battery box. Less visible but equally important features were a special sump guard, tropical cooling equipment, front air line connection and limited slip differential. All in all, the luxurious DAF (typical of many trucks nowadays) was ideal for traversing continents.

One of the most far-reaching moves in co-operation between European manufacturers was the Club of Four initiated in the late 1960s and bearing its first fruit in 1974. This was a joint development programme entered into between Magirus Deutz, DAF, Volvo and Saviem to produce a common range of vehicles for the 6 to 12 ton gross weight truck market, all four companies being involved in joint development, testing and production of parts and components but each maintaining its own company identity for its models. Another even more significant move perhaps was the formation in 1975 of Industrial Vehicles Corporation (IVECO). This consists of the Italian Fiat and Lancia concerns, the German Magirus Deutz company and French Unic concern, which is, of course, controlled by Fiat. The object of IVECO at the time of its formation was stated as follows: 'To offer a wider selection of high quality products and a complete and effective service organisation on international markets; to increase trade between the countries involved in an organisation of European dimensions in such a way as to respond to the industrial and social policies of each country and to the needs for technical progress and competitiveness in the face of international competition'. Fiat is the dominant company, contributing, in terms of US dollars in 1976, 1533 million compared with the 789 million of Magirus Deutz, the 320 million of Unic and the 17 million of Lancia to make up the total IVECO sales turnover of 2659 million.

It was in the 1960s that Eastern European manufacturers started to make themselves evident in the west. Star trucks built in Poland found their way to some of the developing countries, mainly in Africa. Hungary's Ikarus concern started to make an impact on the bus and coach business, but moved forward in the truck sector as well, whilst the Hungarian RABA company went ahead as a result of an agreement to build MAN machines. The German company also sold its expertise to Romania where MAN vehicles started to be produced under the name Roman, a make to be exported in 1977 to Britain, albeit in small quantities. Russia's truck making business developed slowly after the war and it was not until the 1960s that Western Europe saw the first Russian-built trucks being offered through the USSR's state export organisation and companies set up in Western European countries. Today, Russia is selling a few heavy duty dumpers under the Belaz name but the engineering of most Russian designs appears crude compared with modern Western European and US truck-making techniques and, until it improves, sales are likely to be limited.

The Japapese truck manufacturing industry started to make a fundamental impression on world markets in the 1960s, and it was not just complete vehicles that were finding markets. A long term contract in 1968 for Nissan to supply Chrysler in the USA with diesel engines can be seen to be of some significance in this context. This was concurrent with the Japanese in 1967 taking the lead in truck exports away from Britain and the gradual phasing out of many agreements to produce foreign components under licence. Japan's policy of absolute co-ordination of the state and industry with the aim of 'total export' was strongly in evidence in this period, although the results of it were not truly to frighten the European producers until nearly ten years later.

The 1960s saw a tremendous expansion overseas of both European and US truck manufacturers. Whereas British and French companies tended to look to countries which had been within their empires, like Australia and South Africa in Britain's case and North Africa with the French, the German and Swedish truck makers turned particularly to Central and South America. US manufacturers looked further still, not just to other parts of the Americas but to Australia and South Africa in particular where there were obvious similarities to their own distinctive operations.

It is significant that as this policy of establishment by US concerns of factories in overseas territories gathered momentum, the US industry's own direct truck export figures dropped to give Britain the overall lead in truck exports worldwide in 1961.

Right: a type 697NP Fiat 6 × 4 outfit, powered by a 13,798cc, 260bhp diesel, used for aircraft refuelling. Note how again this Italian vehicle is right-hand drive

Probably the most significant development in the establishment of a giant truck-making industry from scratch has taken place in Brazil where the success of locally built Mercedes and Scania heavy duty vehicles in particular and Ford and Chevrolet light commercial vehicles, has attracted heavy investment by Fiat and a more recent venture by Volvo to establish themselves in this market. Today, the Brazilian automotive manufacturing industry ranks in the world's top ten and, in a country larger than the USA virtually without railways except on the eastern seaboard, and totally committed to a road programme the extent of which is unparalleled, the future for the truck is assured.

The main forces at work in the 1970s have been those designed at making heavy vehicles more acceptable environmentally. A big challenge lies in noise reduction. A great deal of work has been done on reducing engine noise by basic design improvements and encapsulation. The Swedish vehicle makers seem to have made the most progress with Volvo's latest designs achieving a low 80–82 decibels. Exhaust emission reduction has also been a major aim and this, too, given proper maintenance, is now achieving the low levels required by governments. Safer vehicles are also a main aim and it is significant that all Common Market truck legislation has this as its first aim.

In 1978, legislation assumes that, environmentally, the internal-combustion engine is supreme, but progress is being made towards obtaining viable alternatives to the petrol and diesel vehicle and certainly in the lighter vehicle classes there could be a swing towards electrics. A main development in battery vehicle use is the Silent Karrier 2 ton payload van developed jointly in Britain by Chloride Technical and Chrysler. This advanced lead-acid battery powered vehicle, built for town deliveries, has a daily range in excess of 100 miles and a top speed of 40mph. Initial service with parcels carriers, dairies, laundry firms, bakeries and stationers suggests it has a promising future especially with oil supplies running low.

Another move of note results from co-operation between Vauxhall and Lucas on the use of the lead-acid battery powered Bedford CF 1 ton van. A number of these went into experimental service in the early part of 1976, and experiments are to be continued in 1978 with a batch of thirty Bedfords being delivered to the Greater London Council. These vehicles have a top speed of 50mph and a daily range of a maximum of 140 miles.

Whether alternative power sources are found or not, however, world demand for road transport for freight is still expanding, and that means good news for the truck for many years to come.

127

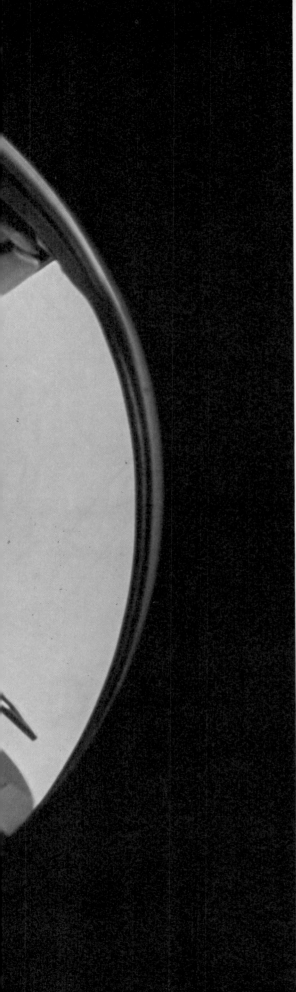

Truckin'

The trucker has always been one of a small band of working class heroes yet, although he has been around since the dawn of the consumer age, it is only comparatively recently that his lifestyle has caught the interest of the general public.

The world of rolling wheels and diesel smoke is complex and wide ranging, and the culture which has evolved around the 'eighteen wheelers' and the people who operate them is all embracing. That special breed of loner who prefers to spend his working life out on the highway can find everything he needs along the roadside. Truckstops supply him with food and fuel, and he is offered the use of a washroom, lounge and sleeping quarters. Late night radio stations broadcast trucker's shows to help him through the night, magazines totally devoted to trucking topics keep him informed and entertained. Along with the development of the American Interstate highway system, and comparable roads in other parts of the world, motor traffic of all kinds has increased greatly. The volume of goods carried by road continues to rise and, as the general public has begun to notice the extent of trucking activity, the public have become fascinated by the fancy custom trucks and the men who keep the big wheels rolling.

The Citizens Band communications revolution has brought millions of Americans into direct contact with the long haul truckers, and most of the fun of CB radio is to be found on the truckers channel 19. Other countries have not embraced CB so extensivley but truck drivers all over the world are basking in the glory of their new found status.

Television shows and numerous magazine features and news stories have brought the truckers lifestyle into the homes of city bound populations in many countries. Publications such as *The Sunday Times* of England, *Der Stern* of Germany, *Playboy, Esquire* and *Rolling Stone* have run major articles on various aspects of the culture.

Truckdriving songs which have been around for many years have recently scored international chart successes, and a steady output of trucking movies throughout the 1970s suggests that this may be a film genre to bring the western type heroic action into the twentieth century.

The United States being the largest consumer and most motorised culture in the world is the home of truck driver mythology, for trucking is about consumption. With the virtual collapse of the railroad network the truck has taken over as *the* means of supply. The highway is now the country's lifeline, and the scope of the road system ensures that any town however small or out of the way can be served.

Across the globe, transportation is developing in the same way. In Europe, Common Market goods are hauled across the numerous

The office of the 1970's trucker is plush, well equipped and safe; and this is just the start of the revolution

borders in TIR trailers which are sealed units exempt from customs inspection while in transit. The massive increase in Arab wealth and spending activity has meant that a whole new trade route has opened up between Britain and other EEC countries and the Middle East. This long haul takes twentieth century drivers into a culture so ancient and alien that in many places there are no roads, just oil drums strung out as markers across the desert, where alcoholic refreshment is definitely not allowed, and where to be involved in an accident might mean immediate imprisonment. This route must remain one of the toughest in the world when cultural conditions are accounted for, but for back breaking, rough track trucking, the struggle across Australia's desert dirt roads by road train 'truckies' would take some topping.

The origins of a trucking culture are right back in the first decades of this century. At that time, railroads served the needs of the worlds population, but the internal combustion engine was beginning to show some of its early potential. In 1910, a truck was sent out on a 3000 mile demonstration run from Detroit, while six years later a GMC truck made the first trans-American crossing. During World War I, the importance of motor transport was made apparent, while during the 1920s and '30s technological developments such as diesel engines, pneumatic tyres and semi trailers helped the truck evolve into an economical and fast distributor of freight.

Better roads opened up areas, particularly in the western states, and, as the hauls became longer, the needs of the drivers were taken into consideration. The Motor Carrier Safety Act of 1935 brought in legislation to control the shipment of road freight and with it came the first of a new generation of sophisticated long haul trucks.

Sleeper cabs and air brakes made the truckers lives safer and more comfortable. Roadhouses began to spring up all over the country at crossroads and on the edges of towns where drivers could stop to eat and chat with their buddies. As the business became more established, the people involved began to speak their own language.

Brakes became known as anchors around 1925 and later became binders; by 1930, the loaders at terminals were dock wallopers; mechanics either hood lifters or just plain maniacs; tyres were donuts or rags, if in poor condition; auxiliary gearboxes known as brownies involved split-shifting, and some sleeper boxes were christened suicide boxes. The growth of the trucking slang vocabulary reflected the establishment of the new sub-culture.

Magazines such as *Commercial Car Journal* advertised the wares of the many truck manufacturers and kept the industry informed, but by the late 1930s the pop media of the day had begun to look to the world of trucking for mass appeal subject matter.

Records with such titles as *Truckers Ball* and *Truck Drivers Blues* were played on the radio, and doubtless on juke boxes in the 'ma' and 'pa' truck stops. In 1940, George Raft, Humphrey Bogart and Ida Lupino starred in the first trucking feature film *They Drive By Night*. Directed by Raoul Walsh, the movie featured Raft and 'Bogey' as brothers and partners in a one truck operation on the West Coast. They run into corruption and, while trying to keep the business going, they do without sleep and crash the truck, costing Bogart his arm. Raft meanwhile goes on to manage a thriving business with the ex-boss's wife and Humphrey is found a place in the garage. The early sequences before the crash show some aspects of the pioneer trucking days, from the hassles of the independent produce hauler to the cameraderie of the late night coffee stop. The time span of the movie takes them from the open sided wooden cabs to the sleek enclosed steel blacktop guzzlers of the late 1930s.

World War II brought another boom for the truck manufacturers with massive production of vehicles in all countries. Hundreds of

Right: the film set and stars of They Drive by Night, Humphrey Bogart, Ida Lupino and George Raft

Below: even though the individual styling of most American manufacturers is similar, their drivers have strong allegiances to each individual make; this is a Diamond Reo wending its way across Arizona

thousands of American trucks were shipped to Europe, Africa and the East, and the necessity for tough and reliable vehicles brought more advances in vehicle technology. On the home front, trucks kept rolling with the materials and parts vital for the war effort.

After the hostilities, mass production and custom building techniques enabled manufacturers to develop another generation of highway haulers, more powerful, safe and economical than before, with the real capability of replacing the rail system. In order to publicise the advantages of the new vehicles, Mack took a Diesel caravan out on the road, and with it a line of promotional toys and novelties such as cigarette lighters, ashtrays and golfballs.

Throughout the 1950s and '60s, as the highways were taking over from the railroads as the bloodstream of America, countless country music artists recorded truck driving songs. Many of these were destined to get no further than the truck stop juke boxes or the midnight-to-six AM

For some time now, trucking has had its own music which is basically country and western with a hint of rock added to give it a 'truck driving spice'. Trucks of course feature heavily on the album sleeves, which range from the sublime to the ridiculous

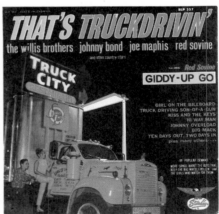

radio shows which were beginning to be heard across the country. Certain small record labels like Starday and King were formed to record local country artists from around the Texas and Louisiana border and their particular 'honky tonk' kind of sound. The chunky rhythms of drums and electric bass and guitar were well suited to the expression of compulsive motion. Among the classic titles recorded in that era, many of which would today be collectors' items, are *Johnny Overlord* by Johnny Bond, *Truck Driving Buddy* by Frankie Miller, *Truck Driving Man* by Hylo Brown, *Diesel Smoke on Danger Road* and *Give Me Forty Acres (to turn this rig around)* by the Willis Brothers. Pedal steel guitar and fiddle arrangements gave emotional support to the sometimes sentimental themes, as in the western swing style numbers of Charlie Moore and Bill Napier who recorded *Lonesome Truck Driver* and *Truck Drivers Queen* among others. Jimmy Logsdon's recording of *Gear Jammer,* a song with a slightly obscure lyric, is one which serves as an

example of how many of these records were produced. The vocal track was generally mixed right up to give prominence to the narrative which was rendered in a distinctive truck balladeer type growl, while traditional treatments of tunes often recur as backing tracks.

With a story to be told, the vocal quality is all important and the first note of the rugged no-nonsense style of a Dave Dudley, Red Simpson, Red Sovine or Jimmy Logsdon song has become a signal to listen out for the story which is bound to unfold – most often with some homespun moralistic conclusion. In fact, some of the biggest hits have been re-citations with hardly any singing.

Outside America there was also a growing public awareness of the role of the truck. In 1955, a movie was made by a French director Georges Cluzot called *Wages of Fear,* which was a suspense thriller concerning the drivers of a nitro carrying truck as they made their perilous way through the South American jungle.

Every country has its own version of the archetypal hero of the road, and the English boys' comic *The Eagle* ran a strip called Knights of the Road which further served to romanticise the lifestyle of the long distance driver, even though the British hauls were short runs compared with those of America and the vehicles the British used were far from luxurious or indeed particularly safe.

Left: In 1955, French director Georges Cluzot made a film about nitro-carrying trucks, Wages of Fear. Here are two stills from the movie

Right: a Peterbilt 'cabover' with a double sleeper

Left: an interesting sign denying truckers' responsibilities for damaging cars at a truck stop. Obviously, cars are not that welcome . . .

Below: an enormous White Freightliner road train; vehicles of this size are not allowed in all states. Note the CB radio antenna and aerodynamic aid on the cab.

Below right: a lady trucker, CB in hand, in the plush surroundings of her White cab. This could be described as either cosy or garish . . .

Overleaf: A 6 × 4 GMC Brigadier looks rather unique with its late 1950s styling in the world of madern day trucking

America's Interstate road system, which was under construction through the 1960s, saw the truckers' stature take another leap in the eyes of populace. Huge oil-company-owned truck stops began to appear and the trucks which pulled up there in their hundreds would stimulate the taste for travel of local youths and impress the touring car driver with their rugged five axle profiles and profligation of out-of-state plates. These truck stops have almost totally replaced the smaller family owned roadhouses as the centre of the truckers' social life. While they often charged more for fuel, they provided many more facilities than the small roadside stops, with lounges, rest rooms, showers, accessory and spares shops. Truck lubrication, reefer unit maintenance and even major overhauls can often be undertaken on the truck stop lot. Many stops also feature truck-washing machines, Western Union wire service facilities and so on.

Although truckers use these facilities regularly, the most frequent excuse for pulling in at a truck stop is for a cup of 'hundred mile' coffee and a smile from a friendly waitress. A lack of human contact on the road does not dampen the truckers' keen interest in the opposite sex – far from it. Some roadhouses calling themselves truck stops don't even sell fuel but rather cater for the male drivers' more physical demands, with such attractions as topless dancers and beer.

Over the last few years, there has been a great increase in the number of lady truckers on the road. Many learn to drive the big trucks so that they can travel with their husbands, but at the same time there are many women who drive with female partners, or even unattached males. Most truck stops now cater for the ladies with special shower and powder rooms and most male truckers are pleased to accept them into their tough and insular world.

When John Steinbeck took to the road to write his *Travels with Charley* in 1961, he made the journey in a truck based camper. As his vehicle was technically a truck he took to using the truck facilities at the roadside and found to his satisfaction that he was accepted by this elite group of professional road users. He discovered that these men had such an insular culture that he could have travelled the whole length and breadth of the United States without ever talking to a local town-bound person. While truckers cruised the highways delivering the goods to all corners of the land, they could exile themselves from the rest of society. Steinbeck liked the truckers he met and often stopped for coffee: 'their great get-together symbol'. The writer appreciated the qualities which enabled these kings of the road to do their job which was not an easy one. For all his conversations with them on his epic journey, Steinbeck concluded that he had only learned enough about the truckers to make him want to know much more.

In the same year that Steinbeck – already an American institution – hit the road, one truck driver was turning in his tire billy and hanging up his ten speed hat to found a magazine which was to become something of an institution to the men who roll the big wheels; Mike Parkhurst was the man and *Overdrive* the magazine. It was the first driver-orientated publication, and the founders intention was to use it as a mouthpiece for the Independent Truckers Association.

With features on political and legislative issues, the magazine kept truckers informed. Pin ups, cartoons and short stories were included for light relief, but one of the biggest attractions was the emphasis on 'gingerbread'. Being published in Los Angeles, *Overdrive* picked up on the car customising craze and began running a regular monthly competition for the smartest and fanciest owner-operator truck. West Coast trucks had always been just that little bit special, with the most expensive being custom built at the Kenworth and Peterbilt factories. They were generally more powerful than the Eastern built rigs, and meant to shine just that little bit brighter. Chrome and stainless steel and polished aluminium were used for bumpers, smokestacks, wheels, air horns, marker lights, mirrors and fuel tanks. Paint jobs got fancier by the year with manufacturers offering multi-colour combinations in chevron or cross-over stripe designs, and interior splendour kits which would put the four-wheeled rods to shame.

Soon, there were several magazines for drivers, ranging from the oil company-owned *Owner Operator* through smaller provincial journals such as *Truck Tracks* from Oregon, and *Open Road* and *Eighteen Wheeler* from Texas. Through these pages, the truckers could read about all the latest developments.

However, the main medium for communication with over-the-road truckers was AM radio which was bringing them an increasing number of specialist shows. These midnight-to-dawn programmes would keep the diesel jockeys awake as they highballed through the night, bringing them a combination of country music, road and weather reports, messages from home and, inevitably, commercials. Most of these commercials were aimed directly at the drivers, and often the independents in particular with offers of return loads, used and new vehicles, truck stop facilities and any of the thousands of accessories and extras with which a truck can be beautified or modified. The stations which broadcast the truckers shows are generally country music stations, most of which are situated in the south and west. One of the most popular is WWL based just outside New Orleans, where Charlie Daniels made his name as the truckers' favourite disc jockey. Nearby, KWKM broadcasts from Shreveport, Louisiana with the *Night Rider Show*; in Los Angeles, KLAC has the *Phantom 570* show and *Truckers Club,* while other stations, from WWVA in West Virginia and KERE in Denver to WLW in Cincinnati

Right: customising takes many different forms; some appear smart, while others are mind boggling

Below: quite a few manufacturers gave their vehicles American Bi-centennial paint jobs as did the Crane Carrier Company of Oklahoma on their 6 × 4 Challenge mixer

and WWOK out of Florida, keep the country virtually under a nightime blanket of truckers shows.

Among the country singers who have specialised in truck driving songs, Red Sovine is one of the most consistently popular, having had hits with such songs as *Phantom 309, Giddyup and Go* and *Freightliner Fever*. Dave Dudley is another growler whose 1963 hit version of *Six Days on the Road* was the first national chart success for a truck driving song. This number has proved to be one of the most frequently covered country songs, with a hard driving rhythm which has been adapted to the style of musicians as different as Taj Mahal and The Flying Burrito Brothers, as well as the countless small time R'n'B groups belting it out in bars and colleges dances even in non-English speaking countries.

In 1965, Dick Curless had the best selling country song of the year with *Tombstone Every Mile*, about a drive along a 41 mile ribbon of ice and the number of victims it had claimed. The folk hero status of the American trucker was improving with every new record which exposed his lifestyle to the general public. The 1968 release *Looking at the World Through a Windshield* by Del Reeves added to the mythology, but stopped short any hopes of complete understanding of the truckers lot with a line about seeing everything in a different light. Non truckers could only guess at what the world really looked like through his experienced eyes.

When many of these songs and other new ones were recorded by long-haired rock groups, youth culture began to embrace some of the redneck

Below left: a Leyland Marathon turbo truck showing how accessible the engine is with the tilt cab

Right: a Saviem artic of 1976 with a trailer which fits on to the kangaroo rail truck system

Below: a good cross section of British middle to heavyweight trucks with, from left to right, a Seddon-Atkinson, a Foden, a Leyland and an ERF

Left: it is always nice to have a female companion with you on the road

Below: reflections at a truck stop in Arizona

Above right: the Super Boss Kenworth and transporter seen at Bonneville salt flats. This Allison-powered drag racer can pull a 14 second quarter mile

Right: horses for courses and trucks for all work. This 130NC Unic is built specially for carrying logs

attitudes, at least in fashions of music, dress and language. A movement looking for the roots of American culture led to bands like the Byrds and Commander Cody's Lost Planet Airmen playing their own styles of country music. Cody's album *Hot Licks, Cold Steel and Truckers Favorites,* released in 1972, had a big influence on the rock/country crossover which the Nashville studios were also aiming at from the opposite direction. The album featured tracks like *Truck Stop Rock, Truck Driving Man, Semi Truck* and *Mama Hated Diesels,* an outstanding song which must have struck some of the more boogie oriented fans as a little weird. It would be easy to think of this song as a parody of the talking-style, home-spun parable, but it was played straight rather than for laughs, and proved to be one of the Airmen's most popular numbers. The band travelled in a customised bus just like the regular country stars and were to be seen and recognised by truckers all over the land. Before they split up in 1976, Commander Cody's band were often invited to play at Nashville conventions, proof enough that they were able to straddle the country culture and the world of rock and roll revival.

The Byrds were another West Coast group who worked their musical way round to country, and they included *Truck Stop Girl,* a Lowell George song on their *Untitled* album. In 1973, ex-Byrd Gram Parsons had an album released called *GP* which was to become a classic example of 'long haired country'. Truck freaks were catered for by the picture which graced the interior of the gatefold sleeve. A handsome California cabover truck trailer rig packed with hay bales is offered as a visual delight and its owner is credited in the sleeve notes. The Flying Burrito Brothers took over where the Byrds left off and recorded many hard driving numbers, including several versions of *Six Days on the Road*; on one album recorded live in Amsterdam it was even featured twice.

Where the pop culture goes, so the mass media follows soon after, and it became 'hip' to look on truckers as the new American heroes, possibly even the last American heroes, or the re-incarnation of the Old West, or even the sailor on the concrete ocean. How the American trucker was romanticised and envied! During the late 1960s and early '70s, when there was a shortage of truck drivers, the romantic pioneering image attracted a lot of new blood to the profession. With the glory came a better standard of living and more respect, but the old time truckers knew there was little new about their kind of heroism and, when compared to the early days of fifty years before, it was a positively easy life.

Far left: Oshkosh, of Oshkosh, Wisconsin, specialise in super-heavyweight trucks. This is their F series 2365 6 x 6 tractor used by the US army for collecting damaged tanks from battle zones

Left: the film Duel was made in 1969 and starred Dennis Weaver and a dirty 'Peter'

Below: an International Transtar 9200 22 wheeler in gravel-carrying guise

There was a certain amount of prejudice against truckers which had probably arisen because of the public's lack of real knowledge of truck drivers as individuals. Very often, they were so high up in the air as to be invisible and motorists in low slung family cars could easily be frightened by the proximity of whining rubber as the big wheels came alongside their windows. Partly because of the roughness of the job and partly due to the self imposed exile and anonymity, there has been a villainous trucker archetype as well as an heroic one. Pictured as sullen, hulky, greasy, beer swilling, speeding, even kidnapping and murdering types, they may be among those who have driven trucks, but they would never make it as professional truckers. A movie made in 1969 exploited the image of the villainous trucker in a way which no other film had done with any villain. The film was *Duel,* the director Steven Speilberg and the contest was between two vehicles – one a small red car and the other a large colourless truck. Throughout the film, we witness the reactions of the car driver as he begins to realise that the truck is out to run him off the road, and fears that there is no way for him to escape it. The truck driver is never seen and to the average motorist it presented the most frightening of highway experiences. Truckers at the time complained that the made-for-TV movie showed them in a bad light, although the point of the movie was more to do with the car drivers' paranoia, with the story depending heavily on irony for its effect. Speilberg went on to direct two of the most successful films ever made, but some film critics consider this to be his best film.

Other films were soon to follow which showed different and more realistic aspects of the highway lifestyle. *Overdrive* magazine produced their own public relations excercise titled *Moonfire,* which showed some of the real problems which beset the modern day trucker as well as his contribution to the community. In 1974, Mark Lester directed a film which was marketed as a soft core skin flick but which could be considered the first hard core truck movie. The plot of *Truck Stop Women* concerns a small team of females who run a truck stop as a front for a hijack and prostitution racket which, not surprisingly, attracts the interests of the mob. The girls play out the roadside breakdown trick in the desert and, as the good natured truckers pull over to assist, they are banged over the head. The trucks are driven back by the girls to the maintenance bay where a couple of Tequila swilling cowboys respray the tractors and re-deliver the trailers. The characters appear real enough to pass as road people, and Lester shows that a big budget is not necessary to get the feel of road dust into a movie. Indeed, the biggest slice of the budget probably went on the stunt driving sequences. Trucks and cars go flying about the screen with satisfying regularity, while the film also packs in plenty of humour, some shootings, beatings and just a little sex. It is a sleazy, entertaining and well photographed movie which suggests that a truck freak was involved somewhere in the making.

Somewhere in the middle of the film, the story line takes a break while Red Simpson sings his song *I'm a Truck* as the musical accompaniment to a montage sequence of trucks rolling across the country. This visual treat features shots from all angles, looking down from bridges, up from the roadside, from the inside lane, the outside lane and the opposite lane and trucks are shown against a variety of skies and landscape backdrops. As a piece of purist trucking cinema, it says more about the movie potential of the eighteen wheelers than most of the so-called trucking plots and stories.

On television, the exploitation of trucks has been less successful. An early TV series, *Canonball,* set the standard and, although it was hardly an inspired series, many of the narrative ideas have since been copied. *Movin' On* attempted to bring contemporary big rig action to the small screen but ended up as a mild afternoon type show. Heroes of regular

series such as *Starsky and Hutch, Gemini Man* and the *Rockford Files* have occassionaly got involved in trucking adventures, but nothing has come close to the real life drama of the open highway.

The development which had the biggest effect on the life of the trucker, and at the same time made his world more accessible to the media and the general motoring public, was Citizens Band radio. CB had been available in the United States since the 1950s and, although it was used by some truck drivers, it was comparatively rare until the oil crisis and the events of 1973. Until the panic over oil supplies, the subsequent shortage, the rising prices and legislation, trucks were generally geared to run at 62 mph. At this speed, they achieved the best overall fuel consumption

Left: a DAF F2800 which is available as either a 4 × 2, 6 × 2 or 6 × 4, with 11·6-litre engines of either 230, 260, 290 or 320bhp, depending on the amount of turbocharger boost

Below: the complete range of 1978 Fiat commercial vehicles

Right: Bedford, the British outpost of General Motors, have recently moved into the heavyweight truck division. This is their TM600 which is powered by a Detroit 8V71 engine

figures. Truckers already considered fuel prices to be too high and, when the speed limit went down in addition to prices going up, they decided to fight. In the winter of 1973, the Independent Truckers Association organised a shutdown. With their LA offices as a base, the independents used CB to spread the word. Most believed that their involvement would bring the country to a stop, and then the truck speed limit would go up and diesel prices would be pegged.

Using the CB radio as a way of organising themselves, the truckers began travelling in company. When running in convoy, the first vehicle, generally the one with the boldest driver or the one with the most pressing

schedule would take the 'front door' and lead a whole convoy of trucks who would be sitting in the 'rocking chair' – that is, having an easy time. The last vehicle in the convoy would be called the 'back door' and his job was to 'rake up the leaves' – keep a check on his tail for any approaching police cars. During the shutdown which took place in the fierce winter months of 1973/4, there were incidents of violence in several northeastern states, and in some cases the National Guard were called out to clear the highways which were blocked by striking truckers. In fact, the shutdown was not successful in its aims, but it did bring a lot of sympathy for the cause of the truckers, and had also demonstrated the value of CB radio. From then on, the sales of CB mobile transceivers took off. Because of the boom in the number of users and particularly those who were using sets without a licence, the Federal Communications Commission dropped the price of a CB licence in March 1975 from twenty to four dollars at a time when applications were doubling by the month. By the end of 1976, there were over six million CB licences in America and the rush on them was so great that temporary permits had to be issued to clear the backlog.

America is still the only country to have taken to CB so readily, although in most countries it is legally acceptable. In Britain, there is no

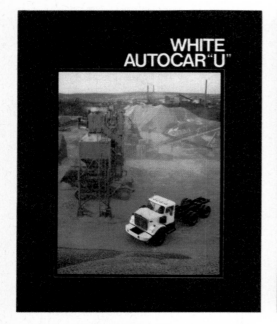

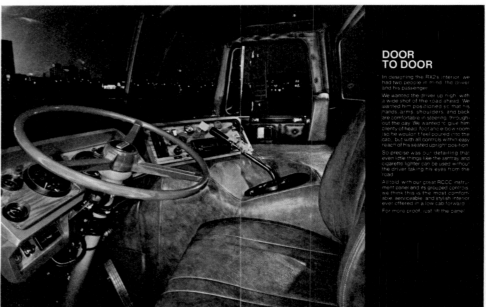

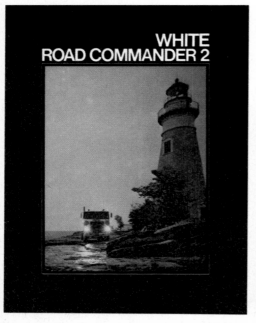

Just like cars, trucks have their own glossy colour catalogues to tempt the prospective buyer. Note the custom paint jobs available with some vehicles

restriction on the purchase of CB radios but to use a transmitter is still against the law unless a Post Office licence is obtained and, as the Post Office has a message-carrying monopoly they do not license two-way-radio communication between untrained citizens. In other European countries, Citizens Band radios using the same 97mHz wavelength are available, although not extensively used, while in Australia they are in use, although technically illegal.

What the CB did for the American trucker cannot be over-estimated. It brought him in contact with his fellow travellers for the first time and relegated those day-long bouts of loneliness to a place in the history books. Where time is of the essence, a truck driver can now make arrangements with maintenance and repair facilities further up the road, and can find his way to the most out of the way freight terminal in a strange town simply by asking for directions over the radio. Any incident on the highway, whether an accident, landslide, heavy snowfall or breakdown, can be reported back to the authorities without wasting time. Many lives and considerable amounts of time and money have been saved by the use CB radio. With millions of four wheel motorists listening in, the world of the trucker, particularly his language and his humour, has become accessible to anybody, and, since the big explosion in CB usage, the

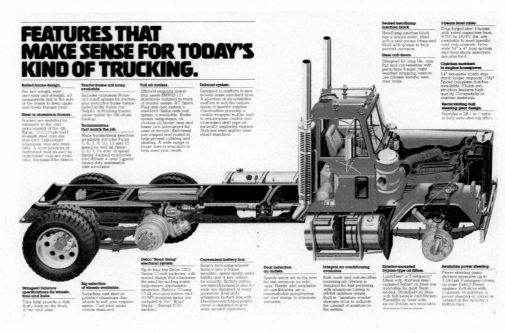

truckers' status has risen even further.

In Europe, there is still something of a negative public reaction to heavy trucks, although material benefits of affluence which every society seems to desire are literally delivered by truck in most instances. It is possible that, if CB radio was available and widely used, much of the guilt-based hostility which masquerades as environmentalism would soon disappear.

In the 1970s, the lot of the European trucker has improved greatly, with the biggest differences coming in the quality of the working environment, the truck cab. Sleeper cabs have made life a lot easier for those drivers who have to rest *en route*. In the days of the two seater non-sleeper cab, truck drivers could frequently be seen slumped over the steering wheel of their trucks or doubled up over the doghouse. The physical and psychological advantages of having a bunk to stretch out on and space to store a change of clothes have done wonders for their social image.

In Scandinavia, where many of Europe's heavy trucks are made, truck drivers were the first to benefit from ergonomic cab design. The image they presented to the world was much smarter and less utilitarian than that of their British counterpart, and mostly due to the better conditions of work. The Swedish Volvo and Scania trucks were the first to offer luxury cabs with living accomodation which, although less roomy than American trucks, gave the long haul man more ammenities.

Above: cabs from a 1965 OM and a 1977 Fiat. In those twelve years, cabs changed from being comfortable but workmanlike to luxurious

Left: before vehicles are put into production, right, they go through rigorous testing. Note the streamlined International in the background

European truckers, once they got behind the wheel of some decent vehicles, began to identify more with their American counterparts; many aspects of their lifestyle were imitated while others could only be wondered at or dreamed of. Magazines sprang up in European countries which were aimed at the drivers, and there was a general exposure to American influence through records and movies.

Even though the CB radio craze did not catch on in Europe, the first smash hit record with a CB theme was truly an international hit, even reaching the top end of the hit parade in England. *Convoy* was recorded by C. W. McCall, alias Bill Fries, director of an advertising agency, self confessed truck freak and shrewd judge of public opinion. The song

brought the truckers CB jargon to a massive audience and the record's success stimulated the American CB boom. The song was based on the events of the shutdown of 1973/4, a real event which McCall exploited to the full.

The movie *White Line Fever* made in 1975 by Jonathon Kaplan developed the CB theme. The hero is an independent trucker trying to carve out a living from the highway who discovers that the big business face of the mob is trying to run his life for him. By way of the CB, he organises a truckers' vigilante group and finishes up by driving his Blue Mule Ford tractor through the glass sculpture which is the corporate symbol of the mob's front organisation.

Other trucking movies followed, with some like *Breaker, Breaker,* being low budget smash-bang efforts for the drive-in shows. *Smokey and the Bandit* was an easy going comedy featuring Jerry Reed as a trucker, and Burt Reynolds as his Trans-Am driving partner. Directed by stunt man Hal Needham, the movie was in the running for America's most popular box office film of 1977.

While *Smokey* was pulling them in, macho director Sam Peckinpah was down in New Mexico shooting the authorized version of *Convoy* with superstars Kris Kristofferson and Ali Magraw, for release in 1978. Although expected to be the definitive blockbuster trucking spectacular, *Convoy* will certainly not be the last of them.

Another box office and critical success personality, Sylvester Stallone, chose to follow on from his famous boxing role with a part in *FIST,* the Federation of Interstate Truckers. This period piece is concerned with a different aspect of the truckers culture. It is the story of Johnny Kovak who started a union back in the 1930s and built it up to become the most powerful and corrupt organised labour force in America.

Still trucking has not been overkilled by the media. Other movies and records are on the way, old ones will be revived and some like *Wages of Fear* will be re-made. As a setting for adventure stories their open road is ideal. Now that the super slab cuts through the wilderness, the freedom of the range belongs to those who travel furthest, but being a trucker means more than living out the western fantasy.

Left: Japanese truck exports have not been on the same scale as their other wheeled vehicles, but Isuzu found that an agreement in 1971 with GM (who would market their vehicles in the USA) helped

Above: the stars of Whiteline Fever, Jan Michael Vincent and Keye Lenz, a film directed by Jonathon Kaplan

The independent trucker who drives his own rig must have mechanical and clerical skills to match his driving ability, for driving is not the whole of it. In that grey area the hero inhabits when he is not on view – his off road time – there are countless obligations to be met. His truck, family, bank manager and bureaucrats of all kinds cry out for action, and it is at times like these that a trucker sometimes cannot transcend his limitations. Then, most truckers would deny their romantic image.

Driving a truck is, after all, a job, and a good one. The erosion of independence in other areas of employment means that driving a truck is one of the few remaining jobs with any dignity which needs no special qualifications.

When the trucker wheels out on to the boulevard, the autobahn or the motorway heading for the furthest corners of the continent, his purpose is clear: the goods must be delivered. However, while he's doing it, he is on his own with his destiny in his own hands.

Running across the Australian desert or through the mountains of Turkey, the trucker is very much alone. The North American continent, however, is trucker paradise with its life-support facilities available along the roadside. Everywhere he sees representations of his own image pointing back at him. Printed plastic ikons, decals, iron-on T-shirt designs, cap badges, belt buckles, cigarette lighters and velvet paintings all carry the image of the trucker. Slogans say: Truck It, Truck Me Baby, Trucking Around, Rather be Trucking and Pulling For the Nation etc. Toy manufacturers sell scale models to make up out of kits or complete models to roll around.

The commercial spin-offs get mixed up with legitimate trade mark symbols such as Cat Diesel, Peterbilt and ThermoKing, which flash from vehicles, badges, patches and roadside neon, thus reinforcing the group identity and stimulating those with a taste for a freer and more mobile lifestyle.

Below: a Fiat nears Karachi on its way from Rotterdam. Here in these dusty conditions the pioneer spirit of the trucker comes out as, in many cases, he picks his own route over the deserts. Here we have the man with his rig and the destination: it may not seem a lot to an outsider but for a trucker it is all he ever wants

Index